Never Be Sick Again by Chad Gonzales is an extraordinary message that arises from the Scriptures and takes us step by step within it to find pearls of the highest content and revelation. It is an opening of the Word and seeing in it how the veil is removed, and one can see in a practical and powerful way what the great truth means under the new covenant of our union with Christ and our full identification with Him, which transcends any other reality and makes us aware that it is our true position, possession, condition, and nature. There we discover our righteousness is from His grace; this means that healing is not something we seek but is Someone who inhabits us. This book is a wonderful, real, and vital answer to questions that all believers have asked ourselves. Reading it with the consciousness of being complete in Him will bring transformation beyond what we have been able to think and imagine.

Ernesto Alemán

Pastor of Palabra y Adoración (Word and Worship)

Christian Church in Bogota, Colombia

Simply awesome! This book by Chad Gonzales will shake you to your core regarding the doctrine of healing. Chad masterfully moves the reader from "trying to get healed" to living in the reality of never getting sick because of the life of God in us. It's bold and revolutionary—and true!

Mark Machen

Pastor of Life of Faith Church and Founder of Forever Free

foreverfree.org

For over a decade, I have gone after and trained others in the ministry of healing with good results. We have eyewitnessed the blind seeing, the deaf hearing, the lame walking, and creative miracles such as large tumors instantly dissolving. Chad Gonzales' books and healing talks have been a great encouragement to us in this pursuit. It is rare for me to meet someone that doesn't just stretch my faith in healing but blindsides me with cutting-edge healing revelation. Chad and his new book, *Never Be Sick Again,* does exactly that!

I had to stop and ponder some bold statements: "Healing is for the sinner, not the saint," and that the "single, greatest mass healing" in history was the Jewish passover. You quickly realize that Chad has given his life to biblical study, meditation, and active participation in healing. *Never Be Sick Again* opened my eyes to a greater "in-Christ" reality that makes me unable to be fully satisfied now with healing a sick Christian. I pray *Never Be Sick Again* would ignite a fire inside you to go after more and not settle for lesser results than the Isrealites had in a lesser covenant. Chad, thanks for forerunning this heavenly revelation and message to the global body of Christ, "Never be sick again!"

Jason Chin
Founder of Love Says Go Ministries and Love Says Go Academy
Author of Love Says Go
www.lovesaysgo.com

Rev. Chad Gonzales is a refreshing voice on the subject of healing. I have known Chad for over 20 years, and he lives what he preaches and has helped countless multitudes see tangible results in the area of physical healing, both in their personal lives and in ministering God's life to others.

Chad's passion for growth and results is contagious, and he has been of great inspiration to me. His messages and personal examples have helped me reach for more and become a more effective minister in the area of healing.

I highly recommend you read *Never Be Sick Again* and elevate your understanding of our covenant with God, our union with Christ, and His life in you, and learn to live in divine health. God has a life for us that is beyond this world, and He wants us to show the world this higher kind of life. This book will help you do just that.

Vidar Ligard
Founder, Safari Mission
National Director, Rhema Bible Training College Kenya

I have known Chad for several years and am honored to call him a friend. He has been consistent and unwavering in his clear communication of God's design and desire for people to be healed and lived healed. In a world of toxic knowledge and deceptive teaching, *Never Be Sick Again* is very fresh, clear, and true. Chad brings a bold and revolutionary message. Each chapter should be read, pondered upon, and thoroughly digested. With our country in the depths of the most horrific crisis of self-inflicted unhealthiness and sickness, we all need to put our faith into action now. I encourage you to take these words seriously, act on them, and then see the Word begin to permeate in your life. *Never Be Sick Again* is a must read (and must share) for everyone. It is my hope this book will be in the "heart and head library" of every pastor and leader. We need to walk in divine healing now!

Drs. Mark and Michele Sherwood
Functional Medical Institute
Tulsa, OK
www.Sherwood.TV

NEVER
BE SICK
AGAIN

Foreword by Daniel Amstutz

Director of Healing Ministry at Charis Bible College

NEVER BE SICK AGAIN

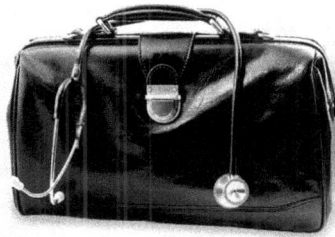

*Access Supernatural Health
Through Jesus' Resurrection Power*

CHAD GONZALES

CONTENTS

FOREWORD

There are so many books about healing but none like this one, because this groundbreaking new book is actually about your union with Christ! Who you are in Him and who He is *in you,* right now, is the root of this book; healing is just some of the supernatural resulting fruit! Jesus came to reveal the Father, and He is so much more than just God with us! Christ in us is the hope of glory, and Chad shows us how that glory is not some fading glory, but as Jesus said in John 17:22 (NKJV), "The glory which You gave Me I have given them, that they may be one just as We are one." Wait, what?

The minute we become a believer, God's presence is forever in us! Because we gave God our "yes," our body becomes the temple of the Holy Spirit. The moment we become a new creation the very image of God becomes ours inside out, and we get a brand-new identity. We have a treasure, but so many don't even know how great this gift really is! His presence is *in us,* so why is so much of the church trying to get into the presence, when Jesus came to get the presence into us? It's the same reason so many are trying to get a healing! They spend a lifetime trying to get what they already have! If only they knew?! Well, now they can know and they will!

It is with enthusiasm that I am recommending *Never Be Sick Again* by Dr. Chad Gonzales. It is an honor to write a foreword for this wonderful new book! I have been waiting for this book to come out ever since Chad came to minister to our entire class of Healing Discipleship at Charis Bible College, where I direct the healing ministry. I'm so excited for you to spend time in this powerful revelation that Chad has received from the Holy Spirit.

This book is a standout in the world of healing books because of the New Covenant revelation and application that it contains. It will challenge you to take a new look into familiar scriptures, because you know faith comes by hearing and hearing by the Word of God. There is a new sound that is coming forth here, and it's a wakeup call!

Don't let what you don't know stop you from what you do know.

As you read and the truth comes alive in you, it comes from God's heart through Chad's years of life experience and seasoned ministry. It's not just a theology or a philosophy for Chad and April!

So much of the church is as sick as the unbelievers, and much of it is because we are trying to get what we already have been given in Christ. It's been so confusing, and sadly, as a result, we have ended up making healing about us!

Chad clearly shows us that it's not about what you are doing! It's about what Jesus did!

Chad takes you on a journey from Genesis through the old covenant, and then he makes a very clear comparison between healing based on your obedience and the healing that Jesus already provided for us based on His obedience.

This book will challenge you with questions like, "Did you know there is no teaching in the new covenant on how to receive your healing?" Or statements like this one: "We teach people that Jesus has already paid for their healing and that it is already theirs, but then we tell them to come up in the prayer line so they can receive their healing."

This book will give you a whole new perspective on what it means to be in Christ, how it applies to your life in your day to day, and how you can make disciples and do what Jesus did!

Let me ask you a question. What would happen if we, as the church, started acknowledging what we already have been given as new creations? What would happen if we really believed that Jesus knew what He was doing when He prayed John 17:21 (NKJV), "That they [we] all may be one, as You, Father, are in Me, and I in You; *that they also may be one in Us,* that the world may believe that You sent Me"?

Healing is not about you; it's *for you!* Greater is He that is in you, and God has so much greater for you and through you. Are you ready?

Chad is a voice for this generation, sounding a clear call to wake up and be part of this third great awakening.

Daniel Amstutz

Director of Healing Ministry at Charis Bible College

INTRODUCTION

You will find a plethora of opinions, perspectives, and beliefs when it comes to the area of divine healing and especially God's will on healing. Some of the most common beliefs concerning God and healing are the following:

1. It is never God's will for people to be healed.
2. God uses sickness to teach/grow/humble people.
3. God's timing isn't always now.
4. You must confess all of your past sins in order to be healed.
5. You must cleanse your generational bloodline.
6. Healing takes great faith to receive.
7. You never know what God is going to do.
8. Sickness is just part of normal life.
9. God provided spiritual healing but not physical healing.
10. Our true healing for the physical body happens when we die.

All of these beliefs and more have not only brought confusion to the body of Christ but they have also hindered people from walking in all Jesus provided for them. Why? These beliefs are not scriptural and have no scriptural backing whatsoever. It's amazing the beliefs people come up with to justify their excuses and lack of understanding instead of simply sticking with the Word.

Although we have received tremendous revelation over the years, we must realize—there is always more. Revelation is always progressive and there is always more when it comes to the Word of God; however, when it comes to our covenant with God, it should be clear and easy to understand from day one.

1

You will find that the gospel message is actually simple and easy to understand—it is just hard for our minds to grasp the simplicity of it and how it could be possible because we have grown up in and among the curse. In the same way that the gospel is simple to understand, so is our covenant with God. God made the old covenant easy to understand and the new covenant even easier to understand; we are the ones who have made it difficult.

One day as I was reading my Bible and meditating on 1 Peter 2:24, the Holy Spirit spoke to me and said, "Go back and study healing under the old covenant because you have a better covenant." I immediately started pulling all of the healing scriptures in the Old Testament and looking at God's covenant with Israel regarding healing. In my utter shock, I began to discover this one thing: the promise of healing under the old covenant was better than the message of healing we have been hearing about for today! Yes, you read that right!

When I began to compare the message of healing that is preached today versus the promise of healing under the old covenant, I found that our modern version was less than what was available under the old covenant. How could that be possible when according to Hebrews 8:6, as Christians, we have "a better covenant established upon better promises"? The answer is very simple: *we have taught new covenant realities from the perspective of the sinner.* How is this possible? Because we do not truly understand who we are—we do not understand our union with Christ. Union with Christ is the distinctive blessing of the gospel dispensation in which every other new creation truth is comprised—righteousness, healing, adoption, sanctification, the future glorifying of our bodies, and many others. When you truly understand who you are, you will truly understand what you have; as a result, you'll stop trying to receive something you have already been made.

SECTION ONE

GOD'S GRACE AND HIS COVENANTS

CHAPTER 1

IN THE GARDEN

In Genesis 1, we find the remarkable story of creation. Starting on day three, God begins creating things that have life in them and that are to produce after their own kind. On day three, He makes all of the plant life with the ability to produce. An oak tree would produce more oak trees and an apple tree would produce more apple trees. On day five, God creates all of the birds of the air and the creatures of the seas, filled with life and the ability to produce after their own kind. Whales would produce more whales, dolphins would produce more dolphins, and all types of fish would produce more of their own. On day six, God creates all the animals on the land as well as mankind. The cattle would produce more cattle, the dogs would produce more dogs, and horses produce more horses. (I'm not sure where mosquitoes came into play. Maybe they were part of the curse that came later!) When God creates man, we see that God gives man life and the ability to produce after his own kind; however, there was the great distinction that only mankind was to be made in the very image of God and then rule over the entire earth.

Genesis 1:26-28 NKJV

> *Then God said, "Let Us make man in Our image, according to Our likeness; let them have dominion over the fish of the sea, over the birds of the air, and over the cattle, over all the earth and over every creeping thing that creeps on the earth." So God created man in His own image; in the image of God He created him; male and*

female He created them. Then God blessed them, and God said to them, "Be fruitful and multiply; fill the earth and subdue it; have dominion over the fish of the sea, over the birds of the air, and over every living thing that moves on the earth."

God made the decision to make man in His image, according to His likeness. Just as with every living creature, mankind was to produce after its own kind; yet, unlike the other living creatures, man was made to live and operate like God on the earth. Man was not God and was totally dependent on God, but man was made in the image of God to live, walk, talk, and rule like God on the earth. Plants and animals were to produce after their own kind and so was mankind, but mankind was also of the Godkind—not God, but given His abilities and filled with His life.

When God made man, He filled Adam with a spiritual substance—the very life that flows in God Himself. The life that flows in God is the same life He put into man. God breathed His DNA into Adam! Man was made in God's image and filled with His life!

Genesis 2:7 NKJV

And the Lord God formed man of the dust of the ground, and breathed into his nostrils the breath of life; and man became a living being.

This spiritual substance, the life of God, was within Adam as a spirit being and was to be God's original immune system for man. This life would flow from the spirit into the body God created in Genesis 2:7.

Now remember, God made man to reproduce after their own kind. Man was made in the image of God to do life like God on the earth. With that in mind, is it possible for God to be sick? The answer is obviously "No." So let me ask you this question: "If it's not possible for God to be sick and He made man to be made according to Him, was it possible for Adam to be sick?" The answer is also an obvious "No."

So, right from the very beginning of creation, we can see that it never was God's will or even intention for mankind to be sick; much less was it even possible for man to be sick. Why? Because God created man to be like Him and do life like Him on the earth. As it is for God in Heaven, it was to be that way for man on the earth!

At this point, everything God had made was good. There was no sin; thus, there was no physical or mental sickness, poverty or fear. There was no disease anywhere because sin was not on the planet and every living thing was connected to life. Everything was good!

The life of God flowed unhindered in man and the light of God was his covering—but that all changed when Adam sinned. When Adam sinned, the curse came upon the earth, and suddenly there was death everywhere. It changed everything from all that you can see and can't see—things changed even down to the molecular level. Not only did Adam's sin affect the world, it affected him as well. We now had a sin problem. Sin was the source and sickness, disease, poverty, depression, mental illness, and host of other issues had now become byproducts.

Adam died spiritually, losing God's life and nature and, as a result, it also affected his body. The life of God which flowed into every cell of his body was now gone. The body, which was completely immune to sickness and disease, was now completely exposed and susceptible to the curse. Man's body was never meant to get old and die; it was only after Adam's sin that it was filled with death. This is why God kicked Adam and Eve out of the Garden so they wouldn't eat of the tree of life—you would have had humanity stuck in a cursed body forever (Genesis 3:22). The body now would have to die. Can you imagine a worn-out, decrepit body that couldn't die? That would be horrible! We are not given any information as to when Eve died, but we know that Adam died at nine hundred and thirty years old. It took a long time for the life of God to eventually get out!

This shows you how much God cares about our body. The skin wasn't meant to lose its elasticity and get wrinkles, and your organs were never meant to give out. Bones were not meant to get weak and the spinal discs shrink. The salvation that would come from Jesus would save the spirit of man, but man would still be stuck in a cursed body and thus never be able to fully walk in all that was spiritually provided. Because of sin and man's connection to it, death was now flowing unhindered; everything that Adam had authority over now had death in it.

Romans 5:12 NKJV

> *Therefore, just as through one man sin entered the world, and death through sin, and thus death spread to all men, because all sinned.*

Granted, before the curse, there was no sickness on the earth for everything was filled with life. However, God in His wisdom and foreknowledge knew Adam's decision and the resulting curse that would come from it. As a result, God created the human body with all of its intricate and fascinating systems, including the human body's immune system. Now, as absolutely amazing our immune system is with communication between the white blood cells, antibodies, and lymphatic system, this was just a backup plan that stemmed from the mercy of God.

For humanity's own good, God Himself escorted Adam and Eve out of the Garden of Eden and away from the tree of life. Genesis 3:24 says God thrust them out and then put an angel to guard the tree of life so no one could ever get to it. If Adam and Eve would have eaten of that tree, we all would have been eternally stuck in spiritual death and never able to have a relationship and fellowship with God like He intended.

God knew the evil that was coming to the world. In order for the plan of Jesus to come to fruition, as well as for people to have an opportunity to grow up and hear about Jesus, humanity would need to be able to make it through life without being ravaged by disease. I personally believe that God made the human body with its immune system as a backup plan for when Adam and Eve sinned. The life of God in man as a spirit being was all we would ever need to sustain life, but when sin entered and thus death, that *zoe* life was gone from the spirit of man and there needed to be a secondary line of defense. This secondary line of defense wouldn't be perfect but was certainly designed to take care of us until a covenant could be made and eventually righteousness be restored.

God in His mercy created the human body with a layer of skin as a first response to keep out disease. He created all of the other systems in the body to work together to fight disease. When you look at what God made, it's just breathtaking. At the moment an infection takes place in your body, your white blood cells jump into action and start removing it. Communication starts taking place at a cellular level to fight off the infection. Even your body getting a fever is your body's innate response at warming your body up so the infection will die.

The immune system is just fascinating, and yet the body, in all of its glory and abilities, which we stand back and look at with awe—this was God's plan of mercy. God never created us to be sick, but God knew the result of Genesis 3 when Adam and Eve would sin. He put these systems in the human body so that outside of the Garden, we would be in a position to receive of Him and be used by Him.

God created the human body with these systems so humanity could ultimately be in a position to be saved and then help others to be saved. The immune system was a mercy system for humanity, not Christianity. God provided this for the just and the unjust because God loves people.

Although God designed a body and an immune system that only the Genius of all genius could design, the immune system alone was subpar compared to what God originally had provided. Before the foundation of the world, God already knew Adam would sell out to satan and so He had a plan in place. As soon as Adam and Eve

9

sinned, the plan of God kicked in—not only to provide eternal salvation, but also to put us in a position to never be sick once again.

Genesis 3:14-15,22-24 NKJV

> *So the Lord God said to the serpent: "Because you have done this, you are cursed more than all cattle, and more than every beast of the field; on your belly you shall go, and you shall eat dust all the days of your life. And I will put enmity between you and the woman, and between your seed and her Seed; He shall bruise your head, and you shall bruise His heel." ...Then the Lord God said, "Behold, the man has become like one of Us, to know good and evil. And now, lest he put out his hand and take also of the tree of life, and eat, and live forever"—therefore the Lord God sent him out of the garden of Eden to till the ground from which he was taken. So He drove out the man; and He placed cherubim at the east of the garden of Eden, and a flaming sword which turned every way, to guard the way to the tree of life.*

As God sent Adam and Eve out of the Garden of Eden, He sent them into a cursed world. It was a world that was now filled with death, and their bodies were now susceptible to the death all around them. Because of sin, death was running through their bodies and there was nothing to stop it.

Romans 5:12-14 NKJV

> *Therefore, just as through one man sin entered the world, and death through sin, and thus death spread to all men, because all sinned—(For until the law sin was in the world, but sin is not imputed when there is no law. Nevertheless death reigned from Adam to Moses, even over those who had not sinned according to the likeness of the transgression of Adam, who is a type of Him who was to come.)*

With every human being born, there was a continuous flow of death because of their connection to Adam. This wasn't God's plan. God made man to be like Him—untouchable by evil because they were filled with life. When you remove life, the automatic result is death, just as when you remove light, the automatic result is darkness. The human body's immune system was amazing, but it wasn't foolproof; it was missing one important ingredient: the life of God. No longer was there a flow of life; in the absence of life, there was now a flow of death into mankind.

Until salvation was provided, man would still be vulnerable to the curse because of their connection to Adam; unrighteousness would always yield physical, mental, and emotional sickness. All of humanity was a slave to sin and thus sickness and disease. Sin was now the master and man was now the slave. As a result, God would need to find a way to legally intervene on man's behalf to provide temporary health until Jesus, the Seed of Eve (Genesis 3:15), could provide eternal righteousness and a divine, untouchable flow of life.

CHAPTER 2

DELIVERED FROM EGYPT

Remember that the Bible tells us in Romans 5 that from Adam to Moses, even over those who had not sinned, death was reigning in their lives. We are looking at a time period of approximately two thousand five hundred years since the sin of Adam. At the time of Moses, we see a major piece of the plan of God come into play. God's plan was to use Moses to bring the Israelites out of Egypt and institute the law—but first, there needed to be a night of miracles.

If you have ever read about the miracles in the Bible, there is one miracle that is probably the least talked about, but is probably the most significant in the area of healing; it is the miracle night of the Passover. In Exodus 12, we find that on the night of the Passover meal, there was a miracle that took place. It was probably the single greatest mass healing that has happened in the history of the earth: at a minimum, hundreds of thousands, possibly over a million, Hebrew slaves were instantly healed of diseases, old bodies were miraculously strengthened, bedridden people rose up, blind were healed, deaf were healed, and paralyzed people began to move as God's healing power swept through the land of Goshen. God was preparing the Israelites, who numbered an estimated one to two million people, for their deliverance from 430 years of slavery (Exodus 12:40).

Psalm 105:37-43 NKJV

> *He also brought them out with silver and gold, and there was none*
> *feeble among His tribes. Egypt was glad when they departed, for*

the fear of them had fallen upon them. He spread a cloud for a covering, and fire to give light in the night. The people asked, and He brought quail, and satisfied them with the bread of heaven. He opened the rock, and water gushed out; it ran in the dry places like a river. For He remembered His holy promise, and Abraham His servant. He brought out His people with joy, His chosen ones with gladness.

When Adam sinned and was sent out of the Garden, the plan of salvation for mankind went into effect. God had raised up Abraham and made a covenant with him to make him the father of the Israelites; but it would be 430 years until they would become a nation and a free people.

The Israelites were about to embark on what was supposed to be a short journey into the wilderness and then into the Promised Land of Canaan; however, the beginning of that journey would take them from Egypt and across the Red Sea. Can you imagine how difficult it would have been to load up people who were sick, lame, and immobile into carts and travel through the wilderness?

Many of these people were weak and sick. Think about what all of the effects of slavery would have done to their bodies. From sunup to sundown, they were doing hard, backbreaking manual labor. They would have had age-related issues, work-related issues, strained backs and muscles, joint issues, and even permanent injuries from their job duties—and this isn't including any common sicknesses or diseases that would have been prevalent all throughout Egypt. The night the Israelites partook of the Passover meal was a miracle night for them! Imagine that possibly over one million people were instantly healed and instantly made strong. Not one single Israelite left Egypt weak or sick, and even the elderly people had their youth renewed!

Through the Passover meal, God was revealing a type and shadow of Jesus as the precious, sacrificial Lamb who was to come—the One who would take care of the sin problem and thus remove all sickness and disease. Have you ever thought about this? The Israelites ate of a spotless lamb, a representation of Jesus, and the result was they were instantly healed and made strong!

Exodus 12:1-13 NKJV

Now the Lord spoke to Moses and Aaron in the land of Egypt, saying, "This month shall be your beginning of months; it shall be the first month of the year to you. Speak to all the congregation of Israel, saying: 'On the tenth of this month every man shall take for himself a lamb, according to the house of his father, a lamb for a household. And if the household is too small for the lamb, let him and his neighbor next to his house take it according to the number of the persons; according to each man's need you shall make your count for the lamb. Your lamb shall be without blemish, a male of the first year. You may take it from the sheep or from the goats. Now you shall keep it until the fourteenth day of the same month. Then the whole assembly of the congregation of Israel shall kill it at twilight. And they shall take some of the blood and put it on the two doorposts and on the lintel of the houses where they eat it. Then they shall eat the flesh on that night; roasted in fire, with unleavened bread and with bitter herbs they shall eat it. Do not eat it raw, nor boiled at all with water, but roasted in fire—its head with its legs and its entrails. You shall let none of it remain until morning, and what remains of it until morning you shall burn with fire. And thus you shall eat it: with a belt on your waist, your sandals on your feet, and your staff in your hand. So you shall eat it in haste. It is the Lord's Passover. For I will pass through the land of Egypt on that night, and will strike all the firstborn in the land of Egypt, both man and beast; and against all the gods of Egypt I will execute judgment: I am the Lord. Now the blood shall be a sign for you on the houses where you are. And when I see the blood, I will pass over you; and the plague shall not be on you to destroy you when I strike the land of Egypt.'"

This was a massive night of miracles that took place because of partaking of the Passover meal, which was symbolic of Jesus. The eating of the lamb would provide instant healing and health for them and the blood over their doors would keep the angel of death away.

The Israelites had a mission to fulfill, and God needed them healthy and wealthy. Not only that, God wanted to show them a better life—a satisfied life in which God was their Provider.

Exodus 15:26 NKJV

> *If you diligently heed the voice of the Lord your God and do what is right in His sight, give ear to His commandments and keep all His statutes, I will put none of the diseases on you which I have brought on the Egyptians. For I am the Lord who heals you.*

In Exodus 15, we find the Israelites have just crossed the Red Sea and watched the destruction of Pharaoh's army. God had miraculously delivered the Israelites out of the hands of Pharaoh and over four hundred years of slavery. The deliverance of the Israelites from Egypt and the crossing of the Red Sea is considered a type and shadow of salvation in the Bible. Very simply, a type and shadow is like a prophetic foretelling of future events in the plan of God. In this case, God is showing us an example of what salvation in Christ would somewhat look like.

God delivers the Israelites from slavery, defeats their former master, and then reveals a marvelous characteristic about their relationship: God is going to be their Healer! The word *heals* is the Hebrew word *rapha*, which literally means "healer, physician of men" (Strong's #H7495). Essentially, God was telling them, "Hey, I want to let you know that from now on, I will be your doctor and keep you healthy!" Think about it: as soon as God saved them, He revealed to them He was their Healer. God could have revealed all sorts of wonderful things about Himself to the Israelites, but He chose to show them they would no longer have to rely on anyone else for healing but Him!

15

This sounds great already but when we read Exodus 15:26 in its full context, we discover this covenant God was making with the Israelites is even better than we thought.

Exodus 15:22-26 NKJV

> *So Moses brought Israel from the Red Sea; then they went out into the Wilderness of Shur. And they went three days in the wilderness and found no water. Now when they came to Marah, they could not drink the waters of Marah, for they were bitter. Therefore the name of it was called Marah. And the people complained against Moses, saying, "What shall we drink?" So he cried out to the Lord, and the Lord showed him a tree. When he cast it into the waters, the waters were made sweet. There He made a statute and an ordinance for them, and there He tested them, and said, "If you diligently heed the voice of the Lord your God and do what is right in His sight, give ear to His commandments and keep all His statutes, I will put none of the diseases on you which I have brought on the Egyptians. For I am the Lord who heals you."*

Most people miss out on the amazing thing God did here when He revealed Himself as their Healer. The Israelites were immediately faced with a dilemma after crossing the Red Sea and entering into the wilderness. After three days in the wilderness, they have no water; then, they get to the waters of Marah, but find it isn't drinkable. So what does God do? God heals the waters.

Do you see it? God wasn't just healing the body. God wasn't healing the problem. *God healed the source of the problem* and then said, "I am your Doctor!"

You have to get this. God wasn't promising to heal their body; God was promising they wouldn't get sick. God was promising that as long as they didn't sin, they wouldn't get sick. God's version of "Jehovah Rapha" was not healing you from sickness, it was healing you from the source of sickness! Jehovah Rapha has been taught as a health insurance program that when you do get sick, God will heal you, but that isn't what God was revealing. This wasn't a health insurance program; it was a disease-prevention program. Health insurance doesn't keep you from getting sick; it's there for when you do get sick. But God was telling them that as long as they didn't sin, they wouldn't get sick. Their lack of sin would allow God to intervene and keep sickness from flowing into their lives.

Remember, the Israelites knew nothing about God outside of the fact that He delivered them through signs and wonders in Egypt and then through the parting of the Red Sea. For over four hundred years, they had lived in a pagan land, full of all sorts of witchcraft, sorcery, and magic. All the Israelites knew were the Egyptians' way of life and reliance on their world systems for survival and living—including in the area of healthcare.

After miraculously saving the Israelites from their enemy and bringing them out with all of the wealth of Egypt, God addresses the other major need in life: health. Have you ever thought about what the two major needs are in life? In life, the two foundational needs are health and wealth. When these two areas of your life are a non-issue, there isn't much that can stop you from achieving your dreams and goals. God immediately took care of the wealth issue and then took care of the health issue. God was revealing that they no longer had to rely on the world's system or the government for their healthcare. God was showing the Israelites that in this covenant He made with them, as long as they did what they were supposed to do, sickness and disease would be a non-factor in their lives!

If you continue reading in Exodus about the grace of God He was bestowing upon the Israelites, we find in Exodus 23 that God's provision of healing was even more amazing than we thought!

Exodus 23:20-26 NKJV

> *Behold, I send an Angel before you to keep you in the way and to bring you into the place which I have prepared. Beware of Him and obey His voice; do not provoke Him, for He will not pardon*

your transgressions; for My name is in Him. But if you indeed obey His voice and do all that I speak, then I will be an enemy to your enemies and an adversary to your adversaries. For My Angel will go before you and bring you in to the Amorites and the Hittites and the Perizzites and the Canaanites and the Hivites and the Jebusites; and I will cut them off. You shall not bow down to their gods, nor serve them, nor do according to their works; but you shall utterly overthrow them and completely break down their sacred pillars. So you shall serve the Lord your God, and He will bless your bread and your water. And I will take sickness away from the midst of you. No one shall suffer miscarriage or be barren in your land; I will fulfill the number of your days.

Do you see how amazing this is? Look at the promise of God regarding their health! As long as they served God and followed His commands, God promised the following:

1. I will bless your food.
2. I will take sickness away from the midst of you.
3. No one will have a miscarriage.
4. No one will be barren.
5. You will live out all of your days.

Now remember: the Israelites were sinners, but they had a covenant with God. They were not saved, righteous, or filled with the Holy Spirit. They did not have a Bible, and they did not go to church. They had been slaves for hundreds of years while living a pagan lifestyle. The normal for their life before God was sickness, disease, poverty, miscarriages, physical issues, unable to produce children, and dying young—much like it is today in our current world. When it came to health problems, they didn't have God to look to for help; their help came from Egyptian medicines and magic. Now, the Israelites were being introduced into a new way of living in their new life with God.

Not only did God promise to be their Healer by stopping the flow of sickness from their lives, God took it up a few notches in this promise: "I will take sickness away from the midst of you!" God tells them, "Not only will sickness not be able to touch you, I will make sure it doesn't even get near you!" God literally promises the Israelites that as long as they serve Him, they will never get sick again, they will never have a miscarriage again, they will be able to have as many children as they want and they will never die young!

Friend, do you see how amazing of a promise this is? And this was part of the old covenant! Imagine being told that as long as you serve God, you never have to be sick again? Imagine being pregnant and knowing that as long as you serve God, this baby in the womb will be born at full term and completely healthy and whole? Imagine being told that being barren isn't possible? Imagine being told that as long as you serve God, you'll never have to be afraid of dying young?

Think about the fears that people live with today in regard to their health. Now think about those fears instantly being removed because you know these instantly become non-issues for the rest of your life. How amazing would that be?

God was showing them what would be available to them under a covenant with Him. The medicines, sorcery, and the doctors of the Egyptians were the only knowledge they had to be healed of diseases, but God was showing them something even better. With His covenant, through their obedience, the flow of death would be temporarily stopped, and as a result, they would be untouchable to sickness or any other health issue and they would never die young.

CHAPTER 3

HEALING UNDER THE OLD COVENANT

As we continue to look at the promises of God to the Israelites, we come to Deuteronomy 7. Here we find some of the same conditional promises of being removed from sickness that were based upon their obedience to their covenant with God.

Deuteronomy 7:12-16 NKJV

> *Then it shall come to pass, because you listen to these judgments, and keep and do them, that the Lord your God will keep with you the covenant and the mercy which He swore to your fathers. And He will love you and bless you and multiply you; He will also bless the fruit of your womb and the fruit of your land, your grain and your new wine and your oil, the increase of your cattle and the offspring of your flock, in the land of which He swore to your fathers to give you. You shall be blessed above all peoples; there shall not be a male or female barren among you or among your livestock. And the Lord will take away from you all sickness, and will afflict you with none of the terrible diseases of Egypt which you have known, but will lay them on all those who hate you. Also you shall destroy all the peoples whom the Lord your God delivers over to you; your eye shall have no pity on them; nor shall you serve their gods, for that will be a snare to you.*

Are you seeing the common language being used under the old covenant promises of healing: "If you do this…then I will do this…." It essentially comes down to the same thing. As long as you do not sin, sickness can't touch you. Why? Sin was the source of the problem. As long as they didn't sin, God was able to keep the flow of sickness out of their lives. Over and over throughout the old covenant, we see the healing promises tied to the Israelites' obedience. In Deuteronomy 7, God tells the Israelites that as long as they listen to and obey His commands, God will keep His side of the covenant, which included the following:

1. God will bless the fruit of your womb.
2. No one will be barren among you or your animals.
3. God will take away all sickness from your midst.
4. You will be financially blessed.

I want you to see what God has done for them because ultimately, this all goes back to the original commission of God found in Genesis 1.

Genesis 1:26-28 NKJV

> *Then God said, "Let Us make man in Our image, according to Our likeness; let them have dominion over the fish of the sea, over the birds of the air, and over the cattle, over all the earth and over every creeping thing that creeps on the earth." So God created man in His own image; in the image of God He created him; male and female He created them. Then God blessed them, and God said to them, "Be fruitful and multiply; fill the earth and subdue it; have dominion over the fish of the sea, over the birds of the air, and over every living thing that moves on the earth."*

I call this the "original great commission." The commission of God to man was, "Be fruitful and multiply; fill the earth and subdue it."

How can you be fruitful and multiply on the earth when you are barren and cannot have any children? How can you go throughout the earth without any money? How can you fulfill this while you are sick? You need health and you need wealth in order to fulfill the commission!

After Adam sinned in the Garden, the curse came upon the earth. As a result of the curse, disease, barrenness, and loads of other bad things came upon the earth, including everyone who was born after Adam.

So this is why God made a covenant with the Israelites. Not only was He showing them their need for a Savior, but God was also putting them in a position to be fruitful, multiply, fill the earth, and subdue it—even though Jesus would not come in His earthly ministry for approximately another 1,500 years! The old covenant was the grace of God to put the Israelites in a position to still fulfill the commission!

In Deuteronomy 28, God gets extremely specific about the blessings and the curses of the law. If there ever were any questions about what was available under the old covenant, this chapter in the Bible answers them all.

Deuteronomy 28:1-14 NKJV

Now it shall come to pass, if you diligently obey the voice of the Lord your God, to observe carefully all His commandments which I command you today, that the Lord your God will set you high above all nations of the earth. And all these blessings shall come upon you and overtake you, because you obey the voice of the Lord your God: Blessed shall you be in the city, and blessed shall you be in the country. Blessed shall be the fruit of your body, the produce of your ground and the increase of your herds, the increase of your cattle and the offspring of your flocks. Blessed shall be your basket and your kneading bowl. Blessed shall you be when you come in, and blessed shall you be when you go out. The Lord will cause your enemies who rise against you to be defeated before your face; they shall come out against you one way and flee before you seven ways.

The Lord will command the blessing on you in your storehouses and in all to which you set your hand, and He will bless you in the land which the Lord your God is giving you. The Lord will establish you as a holy people to Himself, just as He has sworn to you, if you keep the commandments of the Lord your God and walk in His ways. Then all peoples of the earth shall see that you are called by the name of the Lord, and they shall be afraid of you. And the Lord will grant you plenty of goods, in the fruit of your body, in the increase of your livestock, and in the produce of your ground, in the land of which the Lord swore to your fathers to give you. The Lord will open to you His good treasure, the heavens, to give the rain to your land in its season, and to bless all the work of your hand. You shall lend to many nations, but you shall not borrow. And the Lord will make you the head and not the tail; you shall be above only, and not be beneath, if you heed the commandments of the Lord your God, which I command you today, and are careful to observe them. So you shall not turn aside from any of the words which I command you this day, to the right or the left, to go after other gods to serve them.

In this first portion of Deuteronomy 28, God reveals the blessings of their obedience. Look at what all this entails:

1. Your body will be blessed.
2. Your business will be blessed.
3. Your food will be blessed.
4. Favor with the world.
5. Access to the resources of Heaven.
6. Protection from all harm.
7. All that you put your hands to will be blessed.
8. You will be a lender and not a borrower.
9. You will never be slave to another system.
10. The world will be afraid of you because they recognize you are of God.

Now the purpose of the law was to basically show the Israelites that they were sinful people and they needed a Savior (Galatians 3:24), but just because the law couldn't be fulfilled, it didn't mean God was trying to punish them. There is so much grace flowing from God, even in the old covenant! God wasn't trying to withhold His blessings! The law revealed they were not good enough and were unrighteous, but the law also revealed the benefits of the blessing and their ultimate need for a Savior.

God was putting a choice before the Israelites: they could have Deuteronomy 28:1-14 or they could have the rest of Deuteronomy 28—and friend, you don't want the rest of Deuteronomy 28! Look at some of the curses that are listed from Deuteronomy 28:15-68. It's not pretty!

Deuteronomy 28:15-20 NKJV

> *But it shall come to pass, if you do not obey the voice of the Lord your God, to observe carefully all His commandments and His statutes which I command you today, that all these curses will come upon you and overtake you: Cursed shall you be in the city, and cursed shall you be in the country. Cursed shall be your basket and your kneading bowl. Cursed shall be the fruit of your body and the produce of your land, the increase of your cattle and the offspring of your flocks. Cursed shall you be when you come in, and cursed shall you be when you go out. The Lord will send on you cursing, confusion, and rebuke in all that you set your hand to do, until you are destroyed and until you perish quickly, because of the wickedness of your doings in which you have forsaken Me.*

As you can see, the curses were not pretty, but as you continue reading what all the curse entailed, especially in the area of sickness and disease, it gets really bad.

Deuteronomy 28:21-22,27-28 NKJV

> *The Lord will make the plague cling to you until He has consumed you from the land which you are going to possess. The Lord will strike you with consumption, with fever, with inflammation, with severe burning fever, with the sword, with scorching, and with mildew; they shall pursue you until you perish. The Lord will strike you with the boils of Egypt, with tumors, with the scab, and with the itch, from which you cannot be healed. The Lord will strike you with madness and blindness and confusion of heart.*

Beginning in verse 21, we begin to see some details about this sickness and disease that could come as part of the curse. Consumption (tuberculosis), fever, inflammation, boils, tumors, skin diseases, and even mental issues. Notice, these things were not God's will, nor were they supposed to be normal for the Israelites. The covenant God had made with Israel was to put them in a position where these things were to never touch them!

Now, before we go further (and believe me, the health issues with the curse get even worse), I want to make sure you understand that God is not the author of all of these issues. When we read phrases in the Old Testament such as, "The Lord will strike you with boils," we must understand that God is allowing these things, not causing these things. The Old Testament was written in Hebrew and in the Hebrew, these phrases were written in the permissive tense, not the causative tense. God is not bringing sickness and disease upon people; that is what satan does.

Acts 10:38 NKJV

> *How God anointed Jesus of Nazareth with the Holy Spirit and with power, who went about doing good and healing all who were oppressed by the devil, for God was with Him.*

Luke 13:15-16 NKJV

> *The Lord then answered him and said, "Hypocrite! Does not each one of you on the Sabbath loose his ox or donkey from the stall, and lead it away to water it? So ought not this woman, being a daughter of Abraham, whom Satan has bound—think of it—for eighteen years, be loosed from this bond on the Sabbath?"*

Notice in Acts 10:38 and in Luke 13:16 that it was satan who had bound and oppressed people with sickness and disease. Jesus specifically states in Luke 13 that satan had bound the woman with her physical issue. It comes down to this: God will allow what we allow; He will permit what we permit. For God to strike someone with boils, tumors, cancer, COVID, or any other issue, He would be operating in the same arena as satan—and that is not the case. So it is important when we read in the Old Testament, especially regarding disease, that we understand these were things God would permit to happen to the Israelites because of their choices.

Let's continue reading Deuteronomy 28.

Deuteronomy 28:35, 58-61

> *The Lord will strike you in the knees and on the legs with severe boils which cannot be healed, and from the sole of your foot to the top of your head. ...If you do not carefully observe all the words of this law that are written in this book, that you may fear this glorious and awesome name, THE LORD YOUR GOD, then the Lord will bring upon you and your descendants extraordinary plagues—great and prolonged plagues—and serious and prolonged sicknesses. Moreover He will bring back on you all the diseases of Egypt, of which you were afraid, and they shall cling to you. Also every sickness and every plague, which is not written in this Book of the Law, will the Lord bring upon you until you are destroyed.*

Just when you thought it was bad, God tells them in verse 61 that every sickness and disease that is not mentioned will also come upon them until they die! It doesn't get any worse than that! However, when you flip it around, this is amazing news!

Why is that? Because if, under the curse, every sickness and disease on the planet will come upon you, then under the blessing, there isn't any sickness or disease that can touch you! Any disease on the earth, whether written down in the Law or not, it could not touch the Israelites as long as they obeyed God. This certainly would be a motivating factor to obey God, don't you think? You could basically summarize the blessings and the curses into three main areas: health, wealth, and life. If you obey the commands of God, you get all three; if you disobey, you lose all three! For the Israelites, as long as they didn't sin, sickness could not touch them.

I hope you are seeing that even in the old covenant, the Israelites had a choice in what they wanted to experience. As slaves to the curse, God was giving them the opportunity to experience a conditional freedom until Jesus came as the Messiah.

Deuteronomy 30:14-20 NKJV

But the word is very near you, in your mouth and in your heart, that you may do it. See, I have set before you today life and good, death and evil, in that I command you today to love the Lord your God, to walk in His ways, and to keep His commandments, His statutes, and His judgments, that you may live and multiply; and the Lord your God will bless you in the land which you go to possess. But if your heart turns away so that you do not hear, and are drawn away, and worship other gods and serve them, I announce to you today that you shall surely perish; you shall not prolong your days in the land which you cross over the Jordan to go in and possess. I call heaven and earth as witnesses today against you, that I have set before you life and death, blessing and cursing; therefore choose life, that both you and your descendants may live;

that you may love the Lord your God, that you may obey His voice, and that you may cling to Him, for He is your life and the length of your days; and that you may dwell in the land which the Lord swore to your fathers, to Abraham, Isaac, and Jacob, to give them.

Notice this statement: "I set before you today life and death, good and evil." This is all about choice! Even in the midst of being a slave to the curse, the covenant God was providing to the Israelites was giving them their choice back: life or death, sickness or health.

Please don't forget that this is the old covenant we are talking about here. This was a covenant between God and the children of Israel. They were not saved; they were sinners with a covenant based on the blood of animals and a priest who would represent them to God once a year. Despite their sinful state, a major part of their covenant with God was this: "Do what I tell you to do and you'll never be sick a day in your life."

God always wanted His people to be set apart from the world—to be in the world but not of the world. The entire world was subject to disease. How great would it make the Israelites look in the eyes of the world if they had the same experiences as the rest of the world? God's people were always to be "set apart ones"—not just in name, but also by experience.

As we continue looking at God's healthcare plan under the old covenant, we come to Psalm 91, which is a powerful passage of scripture inspired by the Holy Spirit and written by King David.

Psalm 91 NLT

Those who live in the shelter of the Most High will find rest in the shadow of the Almighty. This I declare about the Lord: He alone is my refuge, my place of safety; he is my God, and I trust him. For he will rescue you from every trap and protect you from deadly disease. He will cover you with his feathers. He will shelter you with his wings. His faithful promises are your armor and protection. Do not be afraid of the terrors of the night, nor the arrow that flies in the day. Do not dread the disease that stalks in darkness, nor the disaster that strikes at midday. Though a thousand fall at your side, though ten thousand are dying around you, these evils will not touch you. Just open your eyes, and see how the wicked are punished. If you make the Lord your refuge, if you make the Most High your shelter, no evil will conquer you; no plague will come near your home. For he will order his angels to protect you wherever you go. They will hold you up with their hands so you won't even hurt your foot on a stone. You will trample upon lions and cobras; you will crush fierce lions and serpents under your feet! The Lord says, "I will rescue those who love me. I will protect those who trust in my name. When they call on me, I will answer; I will be with them in trouble. I will rescue and honor them. I will reward them with a long life and give them my salvation."

In Psalm 91, we find the same powerful truths of God's health-care plan under the old covenant. The promises of Psalm 91 can be summed up like this: as long as you trust in Me, you will never be sick again. In verses 6-7, God says, "Do not dread the disease that stalks in darkness or the disaster that strikes at midday. Though a thousand fall at your side and ten thousand at your other side, these evils will not touch you." Imagine being in the midst of a pandemic and people all around you are dying and yet being at rest knowing that the disease can't touch you! Notice: it was not that the *disease won't touch you*; it was the *disease can't touch you!* Imagine if the Church were to walk in that today! Can you imagine what type of witness that would be to the world?

He goes on to say in verses 9-11, "If you make the Lord your refuge, if you make the Most High your shelter, no evil will conquer you; no plague will come near your home. For he will order his angels to protect you wherever you go." Do you see this? *Once again, these are not promises that God would heal them; these are all promises that sickness would not touch them!* No evil can conquer you and no plague will come near your home, and when you do leave your home, His angels will be protecting you everywhere you go! This covenant God made with the Israelites made them untouchable!

As great as this promise was, there is one key difference I want you to notice in Psalm 91 in comparison to all of the prior passages we have looked at in the Old Testament. Before Psalm 91, the promises were based on one condition: do everything I tell you to do. When we get to Psalm 91, the language changes some. Instead of, "If you do everything I tell you to do" it changes to, "If you make the Most High your dwelling place/refuge/shelter." In reality, we see a transition taking place from obedience to trust. Psalm 91 was for the Israelites, but I also believe this was a prophetic psalm looking forward to the new covenant of grace in Christ.

Although we are not given the writer of Psalm 91, I personally believe it was King David himself. When we look at the Old Testament, it is clear to see that David was a type and shadow of Jesus Christ. Both David and Jesus were of the same physical lineage, both of the tribe of Judah, both born in Bethlehem, and Jesus was the fulfillment of God's promise to David that one of his own would be king forever. When you look at the life of David, you can see that he put relationship with God above rules. Because of this relationship and his love for God, David, not only as a king but also as a prophet, declared some very transitional truths regarding God and His covenants. We not only see this in Psalm 91 but also in Psalm 103.

Psalm 103:1-5 NKJV

> *Bless the Lord, O my soul; and all that is within me, bless His holy name! Bless the Lord, O my soul, and forget not all His benefits: who forgives all your iniquities, who heals all your diseases, who redeems your life from destruction, who crowns you with lovingkindness and tender mercies, who satisfies your mouth with good things, so that your youth is renewed like the eagle's.*

In Psalm 103, the psalmist gives us God's benefit package—forgiveness, healing, protection, and provision—and yet this was not a benefit package of the old covenant. Under the old covenant, there was not any forgiveness of sin but only the covering of sin. This was the reason the Israelites had to present themselves once a year for the atonement of their sins (Exodus 30:30). This benefit package was a prophetic declaration of the benefits of salvation by the blood of Jesus Christ.

You could very simply sum it up with one word: *salvation.* The word *salvation* in the Greek means "deliverance, health, safety, protection, preservation, prosperity" (Strong's #G4991). Most people think salvation is just about forgiveness and going to Heaven, but salvation is so much more! There is a direct connection between forgiveness of sin, healing, protection, and provision. We see it in the word *salvation* but also see it in Psalm 103. The reason this is important is because in Psalm 103, we see no mention of the curse or obedience to the law and God's judgments. The very first thing we are told is, "Bless the Lord, oh my soul, who forgives all your iniquities." When forgiveness came, there was a flood of benefits to come!

Not only would healing come because of forgiveness, we are also told our youth would be renewed like an eagle. Have you ever wondered about that? Most eagles molt their feathers once a year. These new feathers allow the eagle to replace worn or damaged feathers so they can stay in top condition. Just because we get older doesn't mean we need to wear out. Remember, Moses lived to be one hundred and twenty years and still had his strength and eyesight. When Caleb was eighty years old, he told Joshua, "I'm just as strong today as I was when I was forty—give me my mountain!"

Joshua 14:7-12 NKJV

> *I was forty years old when Moses the servant of the Lord sent me from Kadesh Barnea to spy out the land, and I brought back word to him as it was in my heart. Nevertheless my brethren who went*

up with me made the heart of the people melt, but I wholly followed the Lord my God. So Moses swore on that day, saying, "Surely the land where your foot has trodden shall be your inheritance and your children's forever, because you have wholly followed the Lord my God." And now, behold, the Lord has kept me alive, as He said, these forty-five years, ever since the Lord spoke this word to Moses while Israel wandered in the wilderness; and now, here I am this day, eighty-five years old. As yet I am as strong this day as on the day that Moses sent me; just as my strength was then, so now is my strength for war, both for going out and for coming in. Now therefore, give me this mountain of which the Lord spoke in that day; for you heard in that day how the Anakim were there, and that the cities were great and fortified. It may be that the Lord will be with me, and I shall be able to drive them out as the Lord said.

How many people in their eighties do you know who are looking for a fight and are still as strong as they were in their forties? But here was a sinner who knew his covenant with God and look at what he accomplished! Should there be something less for those who are children of God? If a covenant with God that halted the flow of sin could provide continued youth, what would a better covenant provide?

In Psalm 103, we are given a prophetic declaration of something coming to humanity that would be far greater than what God had provided under the old covenant. David prophesied of something better and something greater, not because of the covering of sin, but because of the forgiveness of sin through the blood and sacrifice of Jesus Christ.

CHAPTER 4

A BETTER COVENANT

The promise of healing under the old covenant was amazing. Think about it! God's promise was simple: as long as you do what I tell you to do, you will never get sick, never have miscarriages, never become feeble and frail, and never die young. It almost sounds too good to be true, but it was true. Do you know what sounds even crazier? Get this: the Bible says that because of Jesus' sacrifice, we have a better covenant established upon better promises! Because of Jesus, we have something better than Moses, Elijah, David, Solomon, and all of the others who lived under the old covenant.

Hebrews 8:6 NKJV

> *But now He has obtained a more excellent ministry, inasmuch as He is also Mediator of a better covenant, which was established on better promises.*

Now the logical question would be this: if we have something better, why are we not experiencing it? After all, how many Christians do you know who are experiencing the promises of healing at the level of the old covenant?

Have you ever played the telephone game? If you have never heard of it, it is pretty simple. You take a large group of people and line them up. Then, you give the first person a simple message and have them relay it to the next person. This process continues as each person in line relays the message to the person next to them. What happens every single time is that by the time you get to the end of the line of people, you will find that the message has changed significantly. How does it happen? Slowly but surely the message gets slightly altered by each hearer until the last message sounds nothing like the original message. How could it be averted? Simply have the first person share the message every single time. Stick with the source and the message stays pure regardless of time, culture, or location.

Each person hears the message a little bit differently. Just as in the telephone game, this has happened with the message of healing. What started out from Jesus has been relayed by many over the last two thousand years. Instead of the hearer only hearing from Jesus, we have allowed ourselves to hear from multiple hearers, and it has resulted in a muddied message. The "hearing" is affected by experiences, background, perspective, former beliefs, denominations, and a host of other factors.

The message of healing we hear today contains large parts of Jesus' message that makes it sound like Jesus, but just enough of hell's religion to keep you from experiencing what Jesus provided. It only takes a little bit of leaven to spoil the entire lump, and that is what we have today. How do we determine what is true and what is false? We have to lay aside all of our beliefs, experiences, and perspectives and simply go back to see what the Bible says.

CHAPTER 5

THE COVENANT OF GRACE

In Chapter 1, we looked briefly at what God did for the Israelites when He delivered them from Egypt. There are many things throughout the Old Testament that were types and shadows of salvation and yet one of the greatest, in my opinion, is when God saved Israel from Egyptian slavery.

Psalm 105:37-43 NKJV

> *He also brought them out with silver and gold, and there was none feeble among His tribes. Egypt was glad when they departed, for the fear of them had fallen upon them. He spread a cloud for a covering, and fire to give light in the night. The people asked, and He brought quail, and satisfied them with the bread of heaven. He opened the rock, and water gushed out; it ran in the dry places like a river. For He remembered His holy promise, and Abraham His servant. He brought out His people with joy, His chosen ones with gladness.*

What God did for the Israelites was a type and shadow of the new covenant. God delivered the Israelites and made them healthy and wealthy; however, notice the reason:

Psalm 105:42-43 NKJV

> *For He remembered His holy promise and Abraham His servant. He brought out His people with joy, His chosen ones with gladness.*

As part of their deliverance, or you could say "salvation," God healed them. The healing wasn't based on the works of the Israelites; the healing was based on the promise God made to Abraham. Essentially, their healing wasn't based on their works; it was based on Abraham's faith. In reality, this was the grace of God in action, even at the beginning of the old covenant. God was working on behalf of the Israelites because of His promise to Abraham and His Seed.

Genesis 17:1-8 NKJV

> *When Abram was ninety-nine years old, the Lord appeared to Abram and said to him, "I am Almighty God; walk before Me and be blameless. And I will make My covenant between Me and you, and will multiply you exceedingly." Then Abram fell on his face, and God talked with him, saying: "As for Me, behold, My covenant is with you, and you shall be a father of many nations. No longer shall your name be called Abram, but your name shall be Abraham; for I have made you a father of many nations. I will make you exceedingly fruitful; and I will make nations of you, and kings shall come from you. And I will establish My covenant between Me and you and your descendants after you in their generations, for an everlasting covenant, to be God to you and your descendants after you. Also I give to you and your descendants after you the land in which you are a stranger, all the land of Canaan, as an everlasting possession; and I will be their God."*

God made a covenant with Abraham that not only applied to him, but also to his descendants; the land of Canaan, the Promised Land, was part of this promise. However, in looking at the Israelites, we find this covenant with Abraham was not only about material things such as land, gold, and silver, but it also included healing.

Luke 13:10-16 NKJV

Now He was teaching in one of the synagogues on the Sabbath. And behold, there was a woman who had a spirit of infirmity eighteen years, and was bent over and could in no way raise herself up. But when Jesus saw her, He called her to Him and said to her, "Woman, you are loosed from your infirmity." And He laid His hands on her, and immediately she was made straight, and glorified God. But the ruler of the synagogue answered with indignation, because Jesus had healed on the Sabbath; and he said to the crowd, "There are six days on which men ought to work; therefore come and be healed on them, and not on the Sabbath day." The Lord then answered him and said, "Hypocrite! Does not each one of you on the Sabbath loose his ox or donkey from the stall, and lead it away to water it? So ought not this woman, being a daughter of Abraham, whom Satan has bound—think of it—for eighteen years, be loosed from this bond on the Sabbath?"

Jesus' response to the leader of the synagogue revealed that because of her connection to Abraham, she had a right to be healed. God's promise to Abraham was the Blessing—an empowerment to prosper in every area of life.

The Israelites' culture was so far removed from the days of Abraham that the culture and perspectives of Egypt were ingrained in them. All they knew were the gods and practices of Egypt. (How do you think they knew about making a golden calf?)

Before God brought the Israelites across the Red Sea into the wilderness, He miraculously healed them after they partook of the Passover meal. In Exodus 12, God instituted the Passover meal as an everlasting ordinance for the Israelites.

Exodus 12:5-13 NKJV

Your lamb shall be without blemish, a male of the first year. You may take it from the sheep or from the goats. Now you shall keep it until the fourteenth day of the same month. Then the whole assembly of the congregation of Israel shall kill it at twilight. And they shall take some of the blood and put it on the two doorposts and on the lintel of the houses where they eat it. Then they shall eat the flesh on that night; roasted in fire, with unleavened bread and with bitter herbs they shall eat it. Do not eat it raw, nor boiled at all with water, but roasted in fire—its head with its legs and its entrails. You shall let none of it remain until morning, and what remains of it until morning you shall burn with fire. And thus you shall eat it: with a belt on your waist, your sandals on your feet, and your staff in your hand. So you shall eat it in haste. It is the Lord's Passover. For I will pass through the land of Egypt on that night, and will strike all the firstborn in the land of Egypt, both man and beast; and against all the gods of Egypt I will execute judgment: I am the Lord. Now the blood shall be a sign for you on the houses where you are. And when I see the blood, I will pass over you; and the plague shall not be on you to destroy you when I strike the land of Egypt.

I want you to notice this: after eating the unblemished lamb and putting the blood on their doorposts, death and life was taking place throughout the land. While the firstborn of the Egyptians were dying, the firstborn of those covered by the blood were saved. Not only were they saved, again, we find out in Psalm 105 that all of the Israelites were also made strong and whole. I wholeheartedly believe there was a lot of shouting taking place in the Israelite homes; these weren't shouts of sorrow, but shouts of extreme joy. Why? Miracles were taking place while they were partaking of the Passover meal. They were to eat the meal with their shoes on, staff in hand, belt tightened up and ready to leave their enemy, that worldly Egyptian system behind, so they could go to their Promised Land—but they couldn't do it sick, blind, lame, and maimed. There was a whole lot of shouting going on! Over one million Israelite slaves—many with diseases, strained muscles and ligaments, joint pain, permanent disabilities, work-related injuries, and common issues due to age—all of that was instantly healed that night as they partook of the Passover meal.

Don't forget that the Passover meal was a type of what was going to take place through Jesus; Jesus was our Passover lamb. If these miracles happened for the Israelites during the Passover meal, what do you think is possible for those of us under the new covenant of grace?

1 Corinthians 11:23-26 NKJV

> *For I received from the Lord that which I also delivered to you: that the Lord Jesus on the same night in which He was betrayed took bread; and when He had given thanks, He broke it and said, "Take, eat; this is My body which is broken for you; do this in remembrance of Me." In the same manner He also took the cup after supper, saying, "This cup is the new covenant in My blood. This do, as often as you drink it, in remembrance of Me." For as often as you eat this bread and drink this cup, you proclaim the Lord's death till He comes.*

I think we have missed this point, but the "salvation" and healing of the Israelites was not based on their works. This miracle was something that happened to them through their faith in the word spoken by God as well as the covenant God made with Abraham.

Galatians 3:13-18 NKJV

> *Christ has redeemed us from the curse of the law, having become a curse for us (for it is written, "Cursed is everyone who hangs on a tree"), that the blessing of Abraham might come upon the Gentiles in Christ Jesus, that we might receive the promise of the Spirit through faith. Brethren, I speak in the manner of men: Though it is only a man's covenant, yet if it is confirmed, no one annuls or adds to it. Now to Abraham and his Seed were the promises made. He does not say, "And to seeds," as of many, but as of one, "And to*

your Seed," who is Christ. And this I say, that the law, which was four hundred and thirty years later, cannot annul the covenant that was confirmed before by God in Christ, that it should make the promise of no effect. For if the inheritance is of the law, it is no longer of promise; but God gave it to Abraham by promise.

What God did for the Israelites on that Passover night was really because of the covenant God had made for Abraham. In this sense, what God did for them was not based on their works, but based on God's grace. What would come later for the Israelites was the law filled with its blessings and cursings. We have already looked at the healing promises of God under the law, and they are in fact absolutely amazing; and yet, God promised us a better covenant with better promises.

How could it be better? Well for one, the new covenant of healing wouldn't be based on your works; this new covenant wasn't even a covenant made with you—it would be between God and Jesus! Second, the new covenant of healing wouldn't just keep sickness away from you; it provided for you to be completely disconnected from sickness so you would never be sick again.

CHAPTER 6

THE TRUE GOSPEL OF HEALING

One day I was reading Hebrews 8:6 that says, "We have a better covenant with better promises," and I began to think, *If we have a better covenant, we must at least have the best of what is available under the old covenant.*

As I began looking at what was available under the old covenant, I was astonished; it actually sounded better than what was being preached in our modern churches! Under the old covenant, the promise of healing was simple: "Do what I tell you to do and you won't get sick, you won't have miscarriages, you won't be barren, and you won't die young." That sounds pretty good, doesn't it? And yet, we have something better than what the Israelites had under the old covenant. What could be better? Get ready, because it is going to revolutionize the way you see your life.

Romans 5:12-14 NKJV

> *Therefore, just as through one man sin entered the world, and death through sin, and thus death spread to all men, because all sinned—(For until the law sin was in the world, but sin is not imputed when there is no law. Nevertheless death reigned from Adam to Moses, even over those who had not sinned according to the likeness of the transgression of Adam, who is a type of Him who was to come.)*

Notice that death was flowing from Adam to Moses, even over those who had not sinned. For roughly 2,500 years, there was a flow of unstoppable death because of the connection to Adam. People who had done everything right—they still had a flow of death. Why was that? The flow wasn't based on their works; the flow was based on their connection.

Because of their connection to Adam, death was flowing in their lives. You could use the example of an electrical cord. Electricity flowing through the cord has nothing to do with the color, length, or make; it has nothing to do with whether it is being held, being moved, or lying on the floor; the only thing that matters is whether the cord is plugged into the socket.

It was during Moses' time as the leader of the Israelites that God made a covenant with them that included healing. You will notice in our study of healing under the old covenant, sickness was always a possibility if the Israelites didn't obey God. They were an electrical cord plugged into the socket, but you could say that because of their covenant with God, the breaker was flipped. Just as with electricity coming into a house, it flows to the main breaker box and it is present, but if the breaker is flipped, the flow of electricity is stopped to the wall socket—and yet still available to flow at the flip of that breaker.

The old covenant was essentially this: you are plugged into the electrical socket, but as long as you are staying free of sin, the breaker will stay flipped off.

Romans 5:17;20-21 NKJV

> *(For if by the one man's offense death reigned through the one, much more those who receive abundance of grace and of the gift of righteousness will reign in life through the One, Jesus Christ.) ... Moreover the law entered that the offense might abound. But where sin abounded, grace abounded much more, so that as sin reigned in death, even so grace might reign through righteousness to eternal life through Jesus Christ our Lord.*

This is why Jesus' coming was so important—Jesus was coming to change our connection! Because of Adam's sin, everyone was connected to sin and it produced a flow of death. Jesus came to connect us to grace so that life would flow! Because of sin, mankind was unrighteous and thus there was a flow of death; Jesus came to make us righteous so that the life of God would flow eternally! Jesus connected us to righteousness so that grace and life would flow!

Have you ever seen a sinner believe for sickness? Think about it. Where have you ever seen a sinner go around believing to receive sickness? They don't have to believe for it because they are already connected to the flow of death. Well, why would a believer who is connected to a flow of life need to believe to receive healing? You don't have to believe to receive what you already have! Sinners have a flow of death; righteous ones have a flow of life. In reality, the righteous person doesn't need to believe for healing; the righteous person would need to believe for sickness. Why? *You only need to believe to receive what you don't have.*

Romans 6:6-7,10 NKJV

> *Knowing this, that our old man was crucified with Him, that the body of sin might be done away with, that we should no longer be slaves of sin. For he who has died has been freed from sin. ...For the death that He died, He died to sin once and for all; but the life that He lives, He lives to God.*

Notice that we are no longer slaves to sin because we are dead to it. Well, if you are dead to sin, then you are dead to sickness. How is that possible?

It is important that we understand that the sin of Adam and sickness in the world are directly related. Sin is what released the curse into the world. This is why when you read Deuteronomy 28, where God discusses the curse of the law, you will find that much of the curse revolves around sickness. For example, Deuteronomy 28:26-27 talks about being cursed with "the boils of Egypt, tumors, an itch that can't be healed, madness, blindness and confusion." This is just one of many scriptures in which God tells the Israelites about the results of the curse that flowed from sin.

Essentially, sin is the root of the problem and sickness is a byproduct. I say it like this: Sin is the root; sickness is the fruit. When we became one with Christ, God didn't just flip the breaker for us to keep sickness from flowing; He unplugged us from the socket so death couldn't flow anymore! Jesus changed your connection!

God changed your position from being a slave to a master. If you are no longer a slave to sin, you are a master over it. If I am dead to sin, then I am dead to sickness! As a new creation in Christ, I am now the master and I get to choose whether I stay plugged into life or plugged into death.

In Luke 5, we find the story of the paralyzed man who was dropped through the roof. In this story, Jesus equates forgiveness and healing.

Luke 5:17-24 NKJV

> *Now it happened on a certain day, as He was teaching, that there were Pharisees and teachers of the law sitting by, who had come out of every town of Galilee, Judea, and Jerusalem. And the power of the Lord was present to heal them. Then behold, men brought on a bed a man who was paralyzed, whom they sought to bring in and lay before Him. And when they could not find how they might bring him in, because of the crowd, they went up on the housetop and let him down with his bed through the tiling into the midst before Jesus. When He saw their faith, He said to him, "Man, your sins are forgiven you." And the scribes and the Pharisees began to reason, saying, "Who is this who speaks blasphemies? Who can forgive sins but God alone?" But when Jesus perceived their thoughts, He answered and said to them, "Why are you reasoning in your hearts? Which is easier, to say, 'Your sins are forgiven you,' or to say, 'Rise up and walk'? But that you may know that the Son*

of Man has power on earth to forgive sins"—He said to the man who was paralyzed, "I say to you, arise, take up your bed, and go to your house."

Here is a paralyzed man coming to Jesus for healing and instead of dealing with sickness, Jesus tells the man he is forgiven. That seems like an odd thing to say to a man needing healing! However, notice that Jesus equates forgiveness and healing. The Israelite people understood that according to their covenant, if you keep sin out, you keep sickness out. When Jesus said, "You are forgiven," Jesus was really telling the man he was healed. Why? Essentially, you could say that when you remove sin, you also remove sickness. In reality, you could say that how you do forgiveness is how you do healing. This is why we see so many times the relationship between sin and sickness throughout the Bible; where you see one, many times you see the other.

Isaiah 53:4-5 NKJV

Surely He has borne our griefs and carried our sorrows; yet we esteemed Him stricken, smitten by God, and afflicted. But He was wounded for our transgressions, He was bruised for our iniquities; the chastisement for our peace was upon Him, and by His stripes we are healed.

The prophet Isaiah was seeing into the future about seven hundred years and into the spirit realm of what was happening to Jesus. Notice he says Jesus was bruised for our iniquities and wounded for our transgressions; this is simply talking about our sin. Jesus took on the punishment for our sin. Remember, sin was the root of the problem. Jesus died with our sins! Second Corinthians 5:12 says that Jesus who knew no sin became sin, and seven hundred years before, the prophet Isaiah was seeing it take place in the spirit. But notice the result of Jesus taking on our sin: the chastisement for our peace

45

was upon Him and by His stripes we are healed. The word *peace* is the Hebrew word *shalowm*, which means "completeness, soundness, welfare, peace, health and prosperity" (Strong's #H7965). When Jesus took on the punishment for our sin, He also took on all the results of sin, which included sickness. This is why the Scripture says by His stripes we are healed. Do you see it? Jesus was removing the source (sin) so that problem (sickness) would never be a problem again!

Isaiah 53:10 NKJV

> *Yet it pleased the Lord to bruise Him; He has put Him to grief. When You make His soul an offering for sin, He shall see His seed, He shall prolong His days, and the pleasure of the Lord shall prosper in His hand.*

Isaiah continues in verse 10 to show us that God is the one who brought judgment. As a parent, this is tough to read, but you have to look at it through the lens of redemption and ultimately see how much God truly loves you. It pleased God to bruise Him and put Him to grief. The Hebrew word for *bruise* here is *daka* and means "to crush." The Hebrew word for *grief* here is *chalah* and means "to make sick." Essentially, Isaiah 53:10 reiterates what we see in Isaiah 53:5: God made Jesus to be the offering for our sin and the result was Jesus also became sickness. It pleased God to see this happen. Why? Because Jesus was doing this for you and me. Jesus was removing the source of the problem by dying to it.

Throughout the Scriptures, you will find sin and sickness show up together. Notice that when the sin problem is dealt with, the sickness problem is dealt with. When Jesus looked at the paralyzed man, Jesus was dealing with the source of the problem; Jesus put sin and sickness together as a package. The sin of Adam is what released sickness and disease into the earth. Sin is the root; sickness is a fruit. When you remove the source of the problem, you remove the byproduct of the problem!

Psalm 103:1-3 NKJV

> *Bless the Lord, O my soul; and all that is within me, bless His holy name! Bless the Lord, O my soul, and forget not all His benefits: who forgives all your iniquities, who heals all your diseases.*

When forgiveness shows up, healing shows up. When sin is removed, sickness is removed. Without adding to Scripture or taking away from it, you could very easily substitute the word *sickness* anywhere you see the word *sin.* So now read Romans 6 a little differently.

Romans 6:6-7,10 (my rendition)

> Knowing this, that our old man was crucified with Him, that the body of SICKNESS might be done away with, that we should no longer be slaves of SICKNESS. For he who has died has been freed from SICKNESS. For the death that He died, He died to SICKNESS once and for all; but the life that He lives, He lives to God.

In the same way Jesus set you free from sin, He set you free from disease. In the same way you are dead to sin, you are dead to disease. How is that possible? Because when you remove the root, you remove the fruit too! When you get unplugged from the source of sin, the flow of sickness can't flow in you anymore!

Romans 8:2 NKJV

> *For the law of the Spirit of life in Christ Jesus has made me free from the law of sin and death.*

In Christ, I am free from sin. There is a new law that I live according to and it is the law of Heaven: life. What I was connected to, I am no longer connected to. The law that ruled over me doesn't rule over me anymore. Do you know why? Because the law of sin and death is the law of the kingdom of the world. The law of the Spirit of life in Christ is the law of the Kingdom of God! I live from another Kingdom while I am walking through this world. I've been redeemed from the curse of the law and all the demands that were on me (Galatians 3:13). Because I am free from sin, I am truly free from the byproducts of sin, which include sickness.

We see this truth continue on in one of the most well-known healing scriptures in the Bible.

1 Peter 2:24 NKJV

> *Who Himself bore our sins in His own body on the tree, that we, having died to sins, might live for righteousness—by whose stripes you were healed.*

Notice the result of dying to sin leads to healing. Righteousness is now the root, and healing is the fruit. When you receive Jesus as your Lord and Savior, you die to sin, are forgiven of all your sin, and become a new creation. You become the righteousness of God in Christ (2 Corinthians 5:21)! Essentially, you get plugged into a new connection that has a new flow. You get plugged into the Source of life so that all that flows in Jesus flows in you.

Under the old covenant, as long as they did what they were told to do, God flipped the breaker so that sickness couldn't flow through the connection. Under the new covenant, God unplugged you completely! Under the old covenant, God kept it from flowing; under the new covenant, He unplugged you.

Friend, the old covenant provided for the Israelites to never be sick again, yet it was based on their works. The new covenant provided for you to never be sick again, but it's not based on your works—it's based on Jesus' works! Jesus died to sin and because of your union with Him, you died to sin. What Jesus died to, you died to!

The modern Church has preached a message of healing that doesn't truly set the believer free from sickness; *it simply provides good news for when you get sick.* The modern Church teaches you what to do when you get sick, but that is not the gospel of Jesus! *The gospel of Jesus is simple: you'll never be sick because you are dead to it! The gospel of Jesus is not just a health insurance program; it is a disease-prevention program!*

Modern teaching on healing gives you all the steps, keys, 1-2-3s, and A-B-Cs on how to receive your healing, but isn't it interesting that you really don't find any teaching in the new covenant on "how to receive your healing"? The only thing remotely close is found in James 5:14-16 in which the apostle James gives instructions to church leaders on how to bring healing to Christians who are in dire health situations. (We will go into this in much more detail in Chapter 23.) But with all of the teaching we hear today about how to receive your healing, don't you think there would be some teaching on it in the New Testament? Instead of being told what we need to receive, we are repeatedly told what we already have. Why would you need to receive something in the New Testament you have already been given?

1 Peter 2:24 NKJV

> *Who Himself bore our sins in His own body on the tree, that we, having died to sins, might live for righteousness—by whose stripes you were healed.*

Notice that healing is a byproduct of who you are: righteous. Righteousness is not something you are trying to obtain; righteousness is who you are. Righteousness is your identity! Well, the same goes for the byproducts. The apostle Peter is not telling you what you need to obtain; he is telling you who you are: healed.

We must understand God's language of healing. Under the new covenant, when God "healed you," it wasn't healing your body; it was unplugging you from the connection of sin so that life would flow and you would never get sick again!

For too long, we have viewed ourselves as being on defense—as ones always trying to get the ball. Friend, Jesus didn't put you on defense; Jesus put you on offense. Jesus gave you the ball! We have seen the gospel of healing as a promise from Jesus that when we do get sick, He will heal us—but this is not *the gospel of healing*. The gospel of healing is: you will never be sick again! Now certainly, if someone were sick, we know that Jesus is the Healer, but we have lowered the standard of the Healer to being the One who heals the problems instead of the One who healed the source!

Jesus is the Vine and we are the branch. We are connected to Him! What flows in Jesus now flows in us; if it doesn't flow in Jesus, it's not supposed to flow in us!

Remember in Exodus where God revealed He was Jehovah Rapha? Let me ask you this question: did God heal their bodies or the source of the problem? That's right! God healed the waters. God didn't just heal the problem; He healed the source of the problem. He had already healed their bodies on the night of the Passover. Through their "salvation" from slavery, they were completely set free physically and financially.

God did the same thing for us in the new covenant. He didn't just heal our bodies and say, "By His stripes you are healed." No! It's far more than healing our bodies; Jesus removed us from the source of disease, and this is why God sees you as healed! Under the new covenant, God took care of the source of disease: the sin nature. When you became righteous, the sin problem and thus the sickness problem were annihilated! When the sin nature is removed, the sickness nature is removed too.

Isaiah 53:5 NKJV

> *But He was wounded for our transgressions, He was bruised for our iniquities; the chastisement for our peace was upon Him, and by His stripes we are healed.*

Look at what Isaiah saw! As a result of Jesus taking on our sins, it produced healing. When the source is removed, the byproduct is removed too! Righteousness produced healing! When you lost your sin nature, you also lost your sickness nature. How? You took on the very nature of God.

This is why the apostle Paul never specifically addresses receiving healing under the new covenant; although, he does address why Christians do get sick (we will look at this in detail in Chapter 23). Friend, God unplugged us from the connection of death and plugged us into the connection of life.

Why would you need to receive something that was already given? First of all, the Jewish people understood their covenant already included healing and, in Christ, we get an even better covenant! Second, healing was included in salvation. Psalm 91:16 (NKJV) says, "With long life I will satisfy him, and show him My salvation." A long, satisfied, healthy life was part of the salvation package. Why? Because salvation sets you free from the curse! Forgiveness (righteousness) connected you to the healing flow! Salvation unplugged you from the flow of spiritual death, which produced sickness and disease.

You will not find the apostle Paul telling you how to receive your healing; what you will find the apostle Paul telling you is, "As you have received Him, now walk in Him!" (Colossians 2:6). Paul isn't telling you to receive; Paul is telling you to live out what you have already received. When you became a new creation, a new life began—a life in which you never have to be sick again.

CHAPTER 7

THE REAL MEANING OF 1 PETER 2:24

Before we go any further, I want to make this truth very, very clear: we have totally missed the meaning of what God meant when He said, "You were healed."

In Exodus 15, when God said, "I am the Lord your Healer," God wasn't talking about just healing their bodies. In Isaiah 53:5, when God said, "and by His stripes, we are healed," He wasn't talking about just the healing of our bodies. In 1 Peter 2:24, when God said, "You were healed," He wasn't talking about just healing our bodies.

Because we don't fully understand our union with Christ and are still so conscious of the curse, we have viewed God being our healer as, "He heals me when I get sick." Friend, this is not what God meant when He said, "I am Jehovah Rapha." God's version of Him being your healer is not simply providing healing when you get sick. God's version of Him being your healer is that *He healed you from the source of the problem so you never get sick again!*

God told the Israelites, "If you do all that I tell you to do, you will never get sick again, for I am the Lord your Healer." Under the new covenant, we go to 1 Peter 2:24, and it shows us how the new covenant of healing is even better.

1 Peter 2:24 NKJV

> *Who Himself bore our sins in His own body on the tree, that we, having died to sins, might live for righteousness—by whose stripes you were healed.*

Let's break it down.

1. **Jesus bore our sins.** Jesus took care of the sin problem that was the source of all of the issues, including disease. Because of His sacrifice, He put us in a position to have a new connection. No longer would we be connected to the first Adam; now we would be connected to the glorified Christ seated at God's right hand.

2. **We died to sin.** When Jesus died, we died. We identify with His death. When we identify with His death, we are to identify with everything He died to—which includes sickness and disease. We are no longer a slave to sickness; it cannot tell us what to do anymore. Jesus died to the source of it; therefore, we did too. Dying to sin was dying to the source of all sickness and disease.

3. **We live for righteousness.** Jesus became sin so we would become the righteousness of God in Christ. Righteousness is the new position we have. Unrighteousness had us plugged into the first Adam where death was flowing. Righteousness plugged us into Christ where life is flowing.

4. **By whose stripes you were healed.** Healing is the automatic product of righteousness. When sin is removed, healing is the byproduct.

We have viewed "by whose stripes you were healed" as "the scripture to quote when I get sick so I can receive my healing." However, God isn't telling you what you need to receive; He is telling you that because of righteousness, you are completely unplugged from the source of the problem. Righteousness healed you from the source of the sickness, not just heals you when you get sick. Do you see this?

We have taken a powerful truth and devalued it with cursed thinking. Most Christians who read 1 Peter 2:24 will say that "by His stripes you were healed" is talking about spiritual healing. I have heard that definition by all of the critics for years now. Although they are wrong, there is a little bit of truth to it. Now, understand, there is no such thing as spiritual healing. Jesus didn't heal our spirit; He made us brand-new. However, the healing God is talking about—it is spiritual in nature. How is that? Because disease actually is a spiritual thing that manifests physically. I know that may be a hard truth to grasp, but it is true.

Have you ever seen a dead person struggle with sickness? Nope! Do you know why? Because they are dead to it. Dead people do not sin or get sick. Why? Because they are dead. Remember that sin is the source of the problem. If you are dead to sin, which 1 Peter 2:24 tells us that we are, then you are dead to the byproducts. Now this may sound dumb, but you must realize that sin is a spiritual thing; if sin is spiritual, then the byproducts are spiritual. If sin is spiritual, then sickness is spiritual too.

When someone "dies," in reality, they don't die; the body dies—that person simply leaves their body. And yet, the moment that person leaves their body, the sickness stops living and growing. It is a medical fact that someone who has cancer, when they die, the cancer stops growing. Do you know why? Because the spirit of man is gone and sickness is a spiritual thing. When the person dies, the disease dies. The person who was giving life to the body and the disease is now gone!

I remember several years ago I went on a trip to Kenya to interview some current and former witch doctors. The reason I went to interview these men was simply from the standpoint that the spirit realm of the angels is also the spirit realm of the demons. Those involved in witchcraft, although it is absolutely demonic, are still operating in the spirit realm. If we are honest, most of those involved in witchcraft are having greater spiritual experiences than the Christians—this should not be the case. But over the years, I have visited Kenya many times and I knew the power some of these men were operating in was very real; it was a demonic power and a counterfeit power, but a real power nonetheless. I wanted to know what their perspectives and thoughts were on the spirit realm, and thus I spent a week doing interviews with them.

One particular former witch doctor had gotten saved and was now a bishop over nine churches throughout Kenya. I was asking him about his perspective of sickness and he said a few things that really blew me away. He said, "Chad, you must first realize that sickness is spiritual." I told him that I certainly believed that and saw it in scripture, but most American Christians would disagree with him. He laughed and repeated himself, "Yes, but sickness is spiritual—this is why we could make people sick and change the diseases in them." It was at that point, he had my attention. He said, "If people would come to me seeking healing, I couldn't heal them. Satan can't heal anyone. But say they came seeking help with cancer, I would just change the disease to diabetes. They would go away feeling better and the medical doctor would even confirm the cancer was gone, but then a few weeks later, they would start showing symptoms of diabetes or whatever other disease we changed it to. They would think we healed them of the first disease, so they would come back to me and I would just get their money and change it to another disease." I sat there in amazement and said, "How is that possible?" He looked at me and very calmly, yet sternly said, "Chad, I told you that sickness is a spiritual thing."

We see sickness in the physical realm, but it is actually a spiritual thing and this is what 1 Peter 2:24 is talking about. It is talking about a spiritual healing in the sense that God was healing us from the spiritual source, sin, so we didn't experience the physical manifestations of sickness.

If the sin problem has been taken care of, then the sickness problem is taken care of. Jesus became sin and sickness and then died to it. When we died with Christ, we died to what He died to. Because we were unrighteous and alive to sin, sickness could flow unhindered; however, we died to sin and became righteous! What did righteousness do for us? It healed us from the source of the problem: sin. Because we are healed from the source of the problem, the problem is no longer a problem. Righteousness makes you untouchable! Righteousness disconnects you from sin! Righteousness is the new connection in which the only thing that flows is grace and life. Your salvation made you untouchable from all earthly ills.

We have been teaching 1 Peter 2:24 from the standpoint of healing being something that is provided to heal *after you get sick*; friend, that it is an insurance plan. God didn't give us an insurance plan because our covenant makes sickness impossible. The gospel of healing is not health insurance; it is disease prevention! Healing is not a promise; healing is reality. Because Jesus became the chastisement for our peace, we are healed. The sin problem is no longer a problem and, as a result, sickness is no longer a problem either.

God's version of "by His stripes, you were healed" is that you can't get sick because you were healed from the source! It is a new covenant reality that you died to sickness and thus are untouchable in Christ!

SECTION TWO

IDENTITY AND HEALING

CHAPTER 8

THE DAY YOU BECAME ALIVE

One of my foundational scriptures has been 2 Corinthians 5:17. This isn't just a verse to make a good t-shirt with; this is a statement of our brand-new reality and the lens of how I see my life.

2 Corinthians 5:17 NKJV

> *Therefore, if anyone is in Christ, he is a new creation; old things have passed away; behold, all things have become new.*

In the book *Sparkling Gems from the Greek,* Rick Renner teaches that the word *new* is from the Greek word *kainos,* and it describes "something that is brand-new or recently made. It also carries the idea of something that is superior." When you are born again, you are literally born again. In John 3:3, Jesus told Nicodemus that we must be born from above. When we receive salvation, we become something that is not only new, but something of Heaven. You are born of God! You become not only something that never existed before, you become superior to the old you! Now, you may not notice anything different on the outside, but you, the spirit being, became far superior to what you were before you received Jesus. What happened? You became alive!

Jesus talked to the disciples about this in the upper room right before He turned Himself over to the authorities in the Garden of Gethsemane.

NEVER BE SICK AGAIN

John 14:19-20 NKJV

A little while longer and the world will see Me no more, but you will see Me. Because I live, you will live also. At that day you will know that I am in My Father, and you in Me, and I in you.

Sometimes I think we forget about the reality of what the disciples were truly thinking, feeling, and understanding during their times with Jesus. Remember, these are real people who did not understand at the time what we understand right now. These young guys are sitting with Jesus and He looks at them and says, "In a few days, you will become alive." Can you imagine sitting with your friends at a coffee shop and one of them looks at you and says, "Hey! I have good news. In a few days, you are going to live!" You would look at them like they were crazy!

Jesus wasn't talking to physically dead men; He was talking to spiritually dead men—but they didn't understand that! However, Jesus was revealing some incredibly powerful news: you are about to become alive because we are going to become one.

This tells me something—this tells me that spiritually alive people should be different from spiritually dead people. Isn't that the truth with physically dead and physically alive people? There is a tremendous difference! Well, there is a difference between spiritually alive and spiritually dead people too; the only problem is that we have been so small-minded. Church folk have been religiously brainwashed to believe the only difference between spiritually alive and spiritually dead people is that spiritually alive people get to go to Heaven—and try to live better lives while on the earth. People who are one with God and filled with God should have crazily different lives than those who are separated from God and filled with the devil.

Remember, Jesus is looking at spiritually dead men who have been traveling with Him for over three years now and tells them, "You are about to live." So what does this really mean? I'm glad you asked!

Jesus was going to die, and as a result, you and I would become one with Him and experience a supernatural life.

Romans 6:4 NKJV

> *Therefore we were buried with Him through baptism into death, that just as Christ was raised from the dead by the glory of the Father, even so we also should walk in newness of life.*

To me, this is one of the most powerful verses in the Bible in regard to our new identity in Christ. Not only do we identify with Jesus' death, we are also to identify with Jesus' resurrection; yet why would we identify with His resurrection? It is so we can identify with His life! Romans 6:4 tells us that the same new life Jesus lives is the same new life we are to live!

Look at the phrases "just as" and "even so." You don't need a doctorate in Greek studies to understand what these phrases mean. "Just as" and "even so" means very simply: in the very same way. Just as Christ is living a new life, we should also walk in a new life. What does that life look like? It's a sinless life and a sickless life; it is a life that is alive unto God and is flowing with His life. Jesus was raised up and so were we; the only difference is that Jesus knows it and we kind of know it. Friend, what does this new life look like? Our life on earth is to look like Jesus' life in Heaven! As He is, so are we in this world (1 John 4:17)! If Jesus can't be sick, we can't be sick!

Romans 6:6-11 NKJV

> *Knowing this, that our old man was crucified with Him, that the body of sin might be done away with, that we should no longer be slaves of sin. For he who has died has been freed from sin. Now if we died with Christ, we believe that we shall also live with Him, knowing that Christ, having been raised from the dead, dies no more. Death no longer has dominion over Him. For the death that*

He died, He died to sin once for all; but the life that He lives, He lives to God. Likewise you also, reckon yourselves to be dead indeed to sin, but alive to God in Christ Jesus our Lord.

The apostle Paul continues his teaching in Romans 6 letting us know what truly happened through redemption. Notice there isn't anything here about your destination; it's about your new connection. When we died with Christ, we died to sin; we died to the source of the problem. Remember also that where we see the word *sin*, we can substitute it with the word *sickness*. We died to sin. We died to sickness.

Romans 6:7 AMPC

For when a man dies, he is freed (loosed, delivered) from [the power of] sin [among men].

Read it like this: "when a man dies, he is freed from the power of sickness." Now just think about that for a moment. I am free from sickness; I am dead to it. How is this possible? I became alive unto God.

To "become alive" is to get a new connection through salvation. I was dead unto God; now I am alive unto God. What flows in Him now flows in me! The life of God now flows in me as a spirit being, a child of God divinely connected to Him!

To "become alive" is to have unhindered access to the Father. The same fellowship Jesus has with the Father right now is the same access I have right now.

To "become alive" is to be freed from sin. I got unplugged from sin and plugged into righteousness! The root was cut off! I am now grafted into a new root: a root of righteousness! Jesus is the Vine, and I am a branch. What's flowing in Him is now flowing in me! Before salvation, I was connected to a root of sin, and death was flowing in me; now I am connected to righteousness, and life is flowing in me!

Colossians 3:3 NKJV

For you died, and your life is hidden with Christ in God.

The death Jesus died, we died; the life He lives, we live. We must get this! We are looking around at other Christians to show us what our new life looks like. Certainly we are thankful for many of the wonderful examples of upstanding people around us, but no matter how good of a Christian they are, they are not our standard and certainly not revealing our identity. Our new life is hidden with the glorified Christ! Look at Him and see you!

Galatians 2:19-20 NKJV

For I through the law died to the law that I might live to God. I have been crucified with Christ; it is no longer I who live, but Christ lives in me; and the life which I now live in the flesh I live by faith in the Son of God, who loved me and gave Himself for me.

Ephesians 2:4-6 NKJV

But God, who is rich in mercy, because of His great love with which He loved us, even when we were dead in trespasses, made us alive together with Christ (by grace you have been saved), and raised us up together, and made us sit together in the heavenly places in Christ Jesus.

You have to look at yourself in one sense as a dead person to the things of this world. Remember: you died to sin and sickness. Dead people don't sin and dead people don't get sick; you can't see yourself alive unto it anymore. You need to start looking at sickness and say, "You're dead to me!"

You must view sickness as no longer a possibility for you. Why? You are disconnected, and it can't flow anymore. What Jesus is dead to, you are dead to. What Jesus is alive unto, you are alive unto. Go ahead and say it with me: "I'll never be sick another day in my life; it's impossible for me to be sick." You must realize that the day you became alive unto God is the day death died unto you.

Romans 6:10-11 NKJV

> *For the death that He died, He died to sin once for all; but the life that He lives, He lives to God. Likewise you also, reckon yourselves to be dead indeed to sin, but alive to God in Christ Jesus our Lord.*

Jesus made you dead to sin, but He needs you to see yourself as dead to sin; this is why Paul tells you to reckon or consider yourself to be dead to sin. Why do you need to do some considering? Because whatever has your considerations has your faith. If you want to experience what redemption provided, you must change the way you see yourself: you must see yourself as dead to disease. Too many of us are looking at our bodies to tell us who we are as a spirit. Remember, we are to no longer regard ourselves according to the flesh; we regard ourselves according to the spirit. I regard myself as a man in Christ. We must change our perspective of who we are so we understand what we have and thus walk in it.

Remember, you are the righteousness of God in Christ (2 Corinthians 5:21). He didn't just give you righteousness; He made you righteous. This position and condition that you have as a righteous person is not based on you; it is based on who you are in Him. Jesus is perfect and because Jesus united you with Himself, you are perfect too.

CHAPTER 9

MADE PERFECT

After Adam's sin, there was a sin problem. Everyone who was born after Adam was connected to him and thus to the flow of death. In the old covenant, God had set up a way for the Israelites to have the flow of death temporarily stopped as long as they kept their part of the covenant. Within this covenant, God set up the priesthood and sacrifices for which the Israelites would offer sacrifices for their sins and a high priest would offer an annual sacrifice for the sins of the nation.

The covenant was simply a substitutionary measure; as great it was, it still couldn't take care of the sin issue.

Hebrews 10:1 NKJV

> For the law, having a shadow of the good things to come, and not
> the very image of the things, can never with these same sacrifices,
> which they offer continually year by year, make those who approach
> perfect.

Something had to be done about the sin problem so that unrighteous people could become righteous; the answer was Jesus.

When Jesus was in the upper room with the disciples, He prayed a supernatural, prophetic prayer about Himself, the twelve disciples, and us. In this prayer, Jesus revealed the reality of why He truly came.

John 17:23 NKJV

> *I in them, and You in Me; that they may be made perfect in one,*
> *and that the world may know that You have sent Me, and have*
> *loved them as You have loved Me.*

Jesus came to unite you with Him and the Father. Through this union, Jesus made you to be something spectacular; He made you perfect. The Greek word for perfect is *teleioo*, which means "to make perfect, complete, to carry through completely, finish, bring to an end; add what is yet wanting in order to render a thing full" (Strong's #G5048).

The old covenant couldn't fix us; it was simply a temporary patch, but God in His immeasurable grace made us perfect. Righteousness is simply you being made perfect; this is what Jesus came to do! When you became a new creation, you became perfect. When you were made alive unto God, you were made perfect. When Jesus became one with you, it's because you were made perfect. Jesus completed you!

Colossians 2:9-10 NKJV

> *For in Him dwells all the fullness of the Godhead bodily; and you*
> *are complete in Him, who is the head of all principality and power.*

In Christ is the fullness of the Godhead bodily and you are complete in Him. Friend, look at how massive of a truth this is! It is the Father, the Son, the Holy Spirit and you! What does complete mean? Nothing is missing!

Righteousness. Perfect. Complete. Do you realize what that means? There is nothing in you tying you to the curse. The old you is gone. You are no longer connected to the first Adam because you are connected to the glorified Christ. You are connected to the Perfect One! Don't ever forget that the death Jesus died, you died, and the life He now lives, you now live! What Jesus became, you became!

Hebrews 7:28 NKJV

> *For the law appoints as high priests men who have weakness, but the word of the oath, which came after the law, appoints the Son who has been perfected forever.*

Jesus was perfected forever and you were perfected forever. You became righteous (2 Corinthians 5:21). Notice that one word: *forever.* This is about your identity, and there is nothing you can do to change it—even your actions. You were made righteous, perfect, and complete—forever.

Hebrews 10:14 NKJV

> *For by one offering He has perfected forever those who are being sanctified.*

Hebrews 12:23 NKJV

> *To the general assembly and church of the firstborn who are registered in heaven, to God the Judge of all, to the spirits of just men made perfect.*

Why is this important? Because there will be lots of opportunities that come your way to make you think you are not good enough—it is simply the condemnation of satan trying to get you to see yourself outside of your union with Christ (Romans 8:2).

Now some would say, "What if I sin?" I have good news: you were made perfect forever.

I love the fact that the Holy Spirit included the phrase "those who are being sanctified." This means that even while you are working out your salvation, He still sees you as perfect. Even in the midst of your mess, you are still like the Messiah! Even if you sin, it doesn't change who you are. Now this certainly isn't a reason to sin; we should live a holy life. When you understand the grace of God and how much He loves you, you do not want to sin; it's not in your nature anyway! However, this is good news because if you do make a mistake, you are still righteous, perfect, and complete. Notice it is forever; this means nothing you can do will change who you are. Because of your union with Christ, you are forever perfect. When God sees you, He sees you through the Blood of Jesus. He sees you as perfect.

So how does this apply to healing? It is huge! Because even when you sin, you aren't connected to sin, and if you aren't connected to sin, sickness can't flow through you—you are righteous, perfect, and complete! There is a perfect union between you and Jesus so that everything that flows in Him flows in you. You may look at yourself and think, "I don't look perfect, and I certainly haven't lived a perfect life," but this is where you must see yourself as one with Him.

Certainly we will always be growing, but even while I am growing in the things of God, my condition is that of perfection. When I am born again, I am not born a little baby spirit trying to grow up. In the moment I say, "Jesus, be my Lord and Savior!" I am instantly remade into a copy of Jesus, in His perfection and righteousness. I am a full-grown Christ man! Now, I need to grow up in spiritual things, and I do that by renewing my mind and growing in my fellowship with my heavenly Father.

The covenant you have with God is not based on what you have done; it is based on what Jesus has done. It was a covenant made between God and Jesus, but thank God, we got included in it. He made me perfect in Christ so that I could be part of their perfection and be completely removed from sin and thus all of the physical, mental, and emotional illnesses. Because I am perfect, there is nothing standing between me and God when it concerns my fellowship with Him or my healing.

If I as a spirit am perfect, it should affect my body too, because what flows in me should flow through me. I am forever righteous because I died to sin. Because I am the righteousness of God, life flows. I died to sin and was made perfect and filled with His abundant life.

CHAPTER 10

FILLED WITH LIFE

When God created man, He made man in His image and according to His likeness. When God made man, it was good; man was righteous, spiritually alive, and filled with God's life and nature. Man was perfect just like God and, as a result, was able to contain His abundant life; however, when Adam sinned, he died spiritually and lost the life and nature of God.

Genesis 2:15-17 NKJV

> *Then the Lord God took the man and put him in the garden of Eden to tend and keep it. And the Lord God commanded the man, saying, "Of every tree of the garden you may freely eat; but of the tree of the knowledge of good and evil you shall not eat, for in the day that you eat of it you shall surely die."*

Genesis 3:19 NKJV

> *In the sweat of your face you shall eat bread till you return to the ground, for out of it you were taken; for dust you are, and to dust you shall return.*

When Adam disobeyed, he unplugged from the life of God and immediately was plugged into death. It never was God's plan for mankind to die. Death, sickness, poverty, mental issues, depression, addiction—these things were not in the plan of God. God never designed any of these things. All of this and more was the result of the life of God being lost to man. When Adam plugged into death, it produced a flow of sin and sickness into all of those who would be born after him. Thankfully, God had a plan.

Genesis 3:14-15 NKJV

> *So the Lord God said to the serpent: "Because you have done this, you are cursed more than all cattle, and more than every beast of the field; on your belly you shall go, and you shall eat dust all the days of your life. And I will put enmity between you and the woman, and between your seed and her Seed; He shall bruise your head, and you shall bruise His heel."*

God was going to send Jesus to utterly defeat satan and strip him of the authority he obtained from Adam in the Garden of Eden. It was at this moment God's plan of redemption went into effect and God began orchestrating Jesus coming as the Last Adam.

After four thousand years of prophecy about the coming Messiah, Jesus was born. Jesus was 100 percent God, but born 100 percent as a man. Jesus, the last Adam, was sent to fix what the first Adam messed up.

1 Corinthians 15:45 NKJV

> *And so it is written, "The first man Adam became a living being."*
> *The last Adam became a life-giving spirit.*

Jesus came to be a life-giving spirit; He came to put in us what the first Adam lost. How would this be possible? Because God's plan was to go a step further than He did with the first Adam. In the Garden of Eden, man was like God but not one with God, and the covenant

God made was between Him and man. In God's redemption plan, God was going to make a covenant with Himself and unite Himself with us.

If you grew up in church circles where you were told about the Roman road, it was a group of scriptures in the book of Romans that will lead you down the path of salvation. Well, several years ago, when I was studying about the life of God, I found what I call the Road of Life. There are several key scriptures in the book of John that show you God's plan for restoring His life to mankind. It all begins in John 1.

John 1:1-5 NKJV

> *In the beginning was the Word, and the Word was with God, and the Word was God. He was in the beginning with God. All things were made through Him, and without Him nothing was made that was made. In Him was life, and the life was the light of men. And the light shines in the darkness, and the darkness did not comprehend it.*

The word *life* is the Greek word *zoe*, which simply means "the life of God." Every time you see the phrase "eternal life," "abundant life," "everlasting life," it is still *zoe*—the life of God. Jesus is the Word, and this life was in Him. He was sent into the earth filled with the life of God.

The next step on this Road of Life is found in John 5. In this passage, Jesus declares that He is a possessor of the life of God and that He can give it away.

John 5:21,26 NKJV

> *For as the Father raises the dead and gives life to them, even so the Son gives life to whom He will. ...For as the Father has life in Himself, so He has granted the Son to have life in Himself.*

Notice that the very same life the Father has is the very same life that Jesus has in Himself. Because Jesus was a possessor of life, then He could also give it away whenever He wanted to! Friend, you can't give away something you don't have; you can only give what is in your possession. This life was not something Jesus was waiting for or believing for; the life of God was His current possession—it was something He was filled to the full and overflowing with!

As we continue down the Road of Life, we come to John 10:10.

John 10:10 NKJV

> *The thief does not come except to steal, and to kill, and to destroy. I have come that they may have life, and that they may have it more abundantly.*

Have you ever noticed that when people talk about why Jesus came to the earth, they almost always say it was so you could go to Heaven? Certainly there is a Heaven to gain and a hell to shun, but the priority of Jesus coming was not to just get you to Heaven. Jesus didn't come to change your destination; Jesus came to change your position. We were far from God, and Jesus came to unite us with God. Jesus didn't come to just take us somewhere; He came to put something in us: the life of God!

Jesus came that we would have life! How would we actually get this life? It is found in John 17, the last step in the Road of Life.

John 17:20-23 NKJV

> *I do not pray for these alone, but also for those who will believe in Me through their word; that they all may be one, as You, Father, are in Me, and I in You; that they also may be one in Us, that the world may believe that You sent Me. And the glory which You gave Me I have given them, that they may be one just as We are one: I in them, and You in Me; that they may be made perfect in one, and*

that the world may know that You have sent Me, and have loved them as You have loved Me.

As Jesus was in the upper room with the disciples, they partook of the Passover meal. Just as the Israelites partook of the Passover meal and it brought them into a covenant with God filled with promises of health, Jesus' last Passover meal with the disciples was signifying the end of that covenant. It was the end of a covenant with the promise of health and the beginning of a covenant with a reality of health. The words Jesus spoke as He prayed this supernatural prophetic prayer foretold what this new covenant would entail, and it also revealed the purpose of His coming and the cry of His heart: union with man.

Jesus' prayer was that you and I would be one with Him and the Father. Why was union so important? Because God put in Christ what He wanted in us: the life of God. The life of God was the missing ingredient; it was the precious heavenly substance that was God's original immune system. Salvation was not about us going somewhere but about us becoming one with the Vine so all that flowed in Him would flow in us. The gospel of Jesus is not about you in Heaven; it is about Christ in you and His life flowing in you.

Through our union with Christ, His life flows in us—but what does it do? Check out what the apostle Paul says about the life of God in you!

2 Corinthians 4:7-12 NKJV

> *But we have this treasure in earthen vessels, that the excellence of the power may be of God and not of us. We are hard-pressed on every side, yet not crushed; we are perplexed, but not in despair; persecuted, but not forsaken; struck down, but not destroyed— always carrying about in the body the dying of the Lord Jesus, that the life of Jesus also may be manifested in our body. For we who live are always delivered to death for Jesus' sake, that the life of*

Jesus also may be manifested in our mortal flesh. So then death is working in us, but life in you.

Look at what Paul says! Our bodies, these earthen vessels, are carriers of the life and power of God. No matter what comes against it, it can't outshine, outdo, or stop the life of God in us. What is this life supposed to do? The life of Jesus is supposed to affect our human bodies!

This life of God is literally God's original immune system. I truly believe that what we see in existence in our bodies today is literally the mercy of God. Why? Because God loves people, and without it, people would never have much of an existence. The problem is that our natural immune system can only work up to a certain point and then it is overcome with disease—but this was not God's perfect plan. God's perfect plan was the life of God. Why is that? Remember the very first step in the Road of Life?

John 1:4-5 AMPC

In Him was Life, and the Life was the Light of men. And the Light shines on in the darkness, for the darkness has never overpowered it [put it out or absorbed it or appropriated it, and is unreceptive to it].

Darkness can't overcome the light. Light always overcomes, wins, and conquers. The life of God is the light of God. The diseases of the curse cannot overcome the light of God. The life of God is the light in us that obliterates the darkness and disinfects any germ that tries to come against us. The life of God literally put you in a position to never be sick again because it is flowing in you as a spirit being!

I'll never forget in the spring of 2006 when I had my Heaven experience. It was April 1, 2006 when I lay down to go to sleep and, all of a sudden, I found myself in Heaven. Now I certainly don't expect everyone to believe me, but I know what I know. It was like what the apostle Paul said, "In the body or out of the body, I do not know." All I can tell you is that as soon as I closed my eyes, I was there.

The first thing I noticed was not what I saw but how I felt. There was a peace that I had never experienced before; it was the peace of God that surpasses all of your understanding. It was a peace that, honestly, was simply indescribable. The second thing that grabbed my attention was the pulse of electricity that was flowing in my body. The only way I know how to describe it is like if you were to put a TENS (Transcutaneous Electrical Nerve Stimulation) unit on your muscles and you feel the gentle pulsation of the electricity—it was like that, but on the inside of my entire body. I remember standing there on a road with a building to my left and beautiful scenery all around me, but I was mesmerized by what I felt on the inside.

There was a lot more to this experience, but the piece that is pertinent to what we are talking about here is the light that was pulsating through my body. I didn't realize it at the time, but it was the life of God flowing in me! It was only until around 2015 that I began to see the reality of the life of God all throughout Scripture and it astounded me. It led me to writing a book called *Possessors of Life,* and it literally transformed the way I did ministry and the way I saw myself.

God put His life in me to the same degree He has it, and Jesus has it. That life that is flowing through us by our union with Christ—it is in us now and forever. The vast majority of believers know that this abundant life is for the future, but most don't realize it is also for right now to affect our mortal bodies. We have wholeheartedly accepted that forgiveness is a benefit of salvation, but then we stop short. There are more benefits such as protection, safety, and healing. This life is to keep sickness and disease away and keep our youth renewed like the eagle's!

Psalm 103:1-5 NKJV

> *Bless the Lord, O my soul; and all that is within me, bless His holy name! Bless the Lord, O my soul, and forget not all His benefits: who*

forgives all your iniquities, who heals all your diseases, who redeems your life from destruction, who crowns you with lovingkindness and tender mercies, who satisfies your mouth with good things, so that your youth is renewed like the eagle's.

If a covenant with God that halted the flow of sin could provide continued youth, how much more so a covenant with God that completely removed the flow of death? Certainly our bodies get older and will eventually die—but they don't have to die because our bodies wear out; they die because we leave the body. The life of God is to affect your body!

Romans 8:11 NKJV

But if the Spirit of Him who raised Jesus from the dead dwells in you, He who raised Christ from the dead will also give life to your mortal bodies through His Spirit who dwells in you.

In Paul's letter to the Romans, again we find Paul giving us insight into the life of God and our bodies. The greatest display of God's power that the universe has ever seen was on the day He raised Jesus from the dead. When He raised up Jesus, the life of God flowed like it never had before, and yet the same power that was exerted when He raised up Jesus is the same life for your body. Notice this life isn't flowing from Heaven; this life is flowing from the Holy Spirit in you as a spirit being. This means everywhere you go, there is a river of life ready to flow out of you!

When I was a kid, we used to sing this song in church called "I've Got a River of Life." The first verse and chorus goes like this:

I've got a river of life flowing out of me
Makes the lame to walk and the blind to see.
Opens prison doors, sets the captive free
I've got a river of life flowing out of me.

Spring up, oh well, within my soul!
Spring up, oh well, and make me whole.
Spring up, oh well, and give to me that life abundantly.

This was more a kid's song sung in the 1980s, but you talk about a powerful song full of scriptural truth. It's still amazing to me that we sung that song over forty years ago and still the Church has not even believed it—much less put it into action in their lives. Look at the words: where is the flow of life coming from? It's not coming from Heaven; it is coming out of you! We were singing it right, but then when it came to the preaching and the application, we were still waiting on God to pour it out!

The life of God is a spiritual substance that flows in the righteous person. Righteousness is the position of the believer and the condition of the believer. We are complete, perfect, and right! People are waiting for healing power to come out of the sky, but it is actually in the righteous one.

Romans 8:10-11 AMPC

> But if Christ lives in you, [then although] your [natural] body is dead by reason of sin and guilt, the spirit is alive because of [the] righteousness [that He imputes to you]. And if the Spirit of Him Who raised up Jesus from the dead dwells in you, [then] He Who raised up Christ Jesus from the dead will also restore to life your mortal (short-lived, perishable) bodies through His Spirit Who dwells in you.

You as a spirit being are filled with abundant, eternal life—the life that God is and has! Where is that life? The life of God is in you. What will that life affect? The life of God not only changed you as a spirit being, but it flows in you and will affect your mortal body!

Jesus came to give you life and to give it to you in abundance! This life was not only to affect you as a spirit being, but also to affect your body. What is even better, it was not only for your body, but the life of God is there to flow out of you and into others!

Did you notice how many times in the Gospels we read about people trying to touch Jesus? People wanted to touch Him because they knew power was flowing out of Him. Why was this power flowing out of Him? Because Jesus knew He was a possessor of life. This life kept Him free of disease but also healed those who touched Him by faith.

Luke 6:17-19 NKJV

> *And He came down with them and stood on a level place with a crowd of His disciples and a great multitude of people from all Judea and Jerusalem, and from the seacoast of Tyre and Sidon, who came to hear Him and be healed of their diseases, as well as those who were tormented with unclean spirits. And they were healed. And the whole multitude sought to touch Him, for power went out from Him and healed them all.*

Over and over, people were trying to get to Jesus. Why? They did not have this life in them. Because they were connected to the first Adam, they were sinners and connected to the flow of death—but Jesus had a flow of life because He was righteous! As a result, all of the people connected to death needed to touch Jesus because He had a flow of life within Him.

Thankfully, when you and I became one with Christ, we were connected to the same flow. Now as a new creation in Christ, we have that same life flowing in us that is flowing in Jesus. In the same way that Jesus is a possessor of this life, you and I are possessors of this life as well.

At our healing conferences, this a major piece that I push within the services. I want people to know what they have within them. I don't put an emphasis on people coming to me so I can lay hands on them. Although I do lay hands on people if I have to, I push for people to have miracles for themselves right where they are sitting—without anyone touching them. I remember in 2013, I experienced one of the greatest services I have ever been privileged to be a part of; it was a youth camp in Spokane, Washington. One of my best friends, Bryant Hemphill, was the youth pastor of the host church, and he had invited me to speak during the night services. As I was preaching about our union with Christ and this precious life in us, all of a sudden miracles started breaking out. A camp counselor raised her hand while I was preaching and said, "Chad, you have to come look at this!" I walked over, and she pointed at the girl sitting next to her.

This young girl had a skin disease all over her body. However, as I stood there and watched, it was like someone took an eraser, started at the top of her head and slowly just started wiping downward. Suddenly, everyone in the room ran over, and we all just watched this skin disease disappear from top to bottom. The young girl was completely healed in front of our eyes. While we were watching this, teenagers were getting healed all throughout the room. A boy who was legally blind was instantly healed. A girl with a short leg watched it grow out before her eyes. A boy with a torn ACL was healed. A girl with a torn rotator cuff was healed. It was amazing hearing all of the healing testimonies that took place all throughout the night.

That is the way I like to see our healing services and conferences take place. Do you know why these things happen? Because I put the emphasis on what they have within them—not on what they need to get. Once they understand what they have within them, then it makes it even easier for them to release it to others just like Jesus!

Recently, April and I were in Puerto Rico holding a conference. I was teaching about the life of God in us and we saw miracles break out. Before the service was over, this one particular woman had to leave a little early. She said she had a serious back and shoulder problem, but as she was in the parking lot walking to her car, she got healed. She felt a warmth come over her, and all of the pain disappeared, and her full range of motion came back! While she was in the parking lot, we had begun to minister to various people in the congregation. There was a young woman in her early twenties who had severely injured her ankle. It was black and blue with bruising and very swollen, and she hobbled around on it with the aid of crutches. April and I laid our hands on her and released the life of God into it. April then grabbed her hand and they began to walk. As they began to walk, you could see it in the young woman's eyes: there was no more pain. She let go of April's hand and started running, jumping and dancing! She was a dancer, and she had a recital the next day; she was so excited that she was now going to be able to participate! That was great, but the story gets even better! While April and the woman were walking across the front of the auditorium, as they passed some of the people, there were some teenage boys who had ankle and knee injuries and were instantly healed as April and the woman walked in front of them! The life of God was flowing!

Don't ever forget that righteous people are filled with life. It is not about you; it is about Who you are connected to. The more we know, the more it will flow. The more conscious we become of what we have, the more we will see it flow in us and through us. When you understand your position in Christ, you will understand your possessions in Christ—and one of those precious, priceless possessions is the life of God.

CHAPTER 11

THE FLOW IN YOU

It's important to understand that you are a three-part being; you are a spirit, you have a soul (your mind, will, and emotions), and you live in your body. God created us in a way that you, the spirit, would be in control of the other parts. God made it so the spirit is not only to dominate the body, but also that the contents of our spirit would affect our body. In the beginning of creation, God created man in His image and likeness. Then in Genesis 2, we see something extraordinary take place.

Genesis 2:7 NKJV

> *And the Lord God formed man of the dust of the ground, and breathed into his nostrils the breath of life; and man became a living being.*

God not only created man to act like Him, look like Him, and think like Him, God also designed and called man to live like Him—and then gave man the equipment to make it possible: the life of God. The Bible tells us that God breathed life into man and man became a living being. I want to point out that man's body was lying dormant and inactive; there was no motion, no activity, and no life produced from the body until the life of God entered. God placed man's spirit, which was filled to the full of eternal life, into the body of man. As soon as the life of God entered the body, the body became

NEVER BE SICK AGAIN

alive. Notice that the body responded to the spirit—not the other way around.

Friend, God designed your body to be a slave to you as a spirit! Your body can't fully do its job without the life of God. Your body is instinctively trying to heal itself, but for your body to work the way God designed for it to work, it needs that heavenly substance flowing in every cell of your being. We have already seen how Adam lost the life of God and how Jesus came to get it back for us. Let's look at some examples with Jesus. Then, I want you to see what the Word of God has to say about this wonderful life from Heaven that resides in you as a spirit.

John 4:9-14 NKJV

> *Then the woman of Samaria said to Him, "How is it that You, being a Jew, ask a drink from me, a Samaritan woman?" For Jews have no dealings with Samaritans. Jesus answered and said to her, "If you knew the gift of God, and who it is who says to you, 'Give Me a drink,' you would have asked Him, and He would have given you living water." The woman said to Him, "Sir, You have nothing to draw with, and the well is deep. Where then do You get that living water? Are You greater than our father Jacob, who gave us the well, and drank from it himself, as well as his sons and his livestock?" Jesus answered and said to her, "Whoever drinks of this water will thirst again, but whoever drinks of the water that I shall give him will never thirst. But the water that I shall give him will become in him a fountain of water springing up into everlasting life."*

As Jesus is speaking with the Samaritan woman, He makes a statement about healing that most people miss. Jesus says, "The water I give will become in him a fountain springing up into everlasting life." Jesus is talking about the life of God here; there are three nuggets I want you to see in this statement. Number one, Jesus said, "The water I give." This spiritual substance was something Jesus was giving to us. This wasn't something that would be given repeatedly; this was a one-time gift. Number two, this spiritual substance was not a gift to be placed in your hands; this was something to be placed into your spirit. Number three, this substance in your spirit would be a continual fountain from which life would flow!

John 7:38 NKJV

> *He who believes in Me, as the Scripture has said, out of his heart will flow rivers of living water.*

John 7:38 TPT

> *Believe in me so that rivers of living water will burst out from within you, flowing from your innermost being, just like the Scripture says!*

Jesus is not only talking about salvation, but also about divine health. The plan of God was that through salvation, the life of God would flow into us as a spirit and be a continual flow of healing and health into our body and into others. This was God's plan in the Garden of Eden and the plan has never changed. Remember, God put this life into Jesus, and Jesus came so we could experience this life abundantly!

Friend, here is a powerful revelation for you: as a Christian, you no longer have to ask God to heal you! Don't believe me? Let's look at more Scripture! In Ephesians 1, the apostle Paul gives us a prayer he prayed continually for the Church.

Ephesians 1:15-21 NKJV

> *Therefore I also, after I heard of your faith in the Lord Jesus and your love for all the saints, do not cease to give thanks for you, making mention of you in my prayers: that the God of our Lord Jesus*

> *Christ, the Father of glory, may give to you the spirit of wisdom and revelation in the knowledge of Him, the eyes of your understanding being enlightened; that you may know what is the hope of His calling, what are the riches of the glory of His inheritance in the saints, and what is the exceeding greatness of His power toward us who believe, according to the working of His mighty power which He worked in Christ when He raised Him from the dead and seated Him at His right hand in the heavenly places, far above all principality and power and might and dominion, and every name that is named, not only in this age but also in that which is to come.*

Paul prayed for God to give us one thing: revelation. Why? Because Paul wanted us to understand what God had already given us. What was one of the things God had already given us through our union with Christ? The same power that raised Jesus from the dead! We also see it in Romans 8:11.

Romans 8:11 NKJV

> *But if the Spirit of Him who raised Jesus from the dead dwells in you, He who raised Christ from the dead will also give life to your mortal bodies through His Spirit who dwells in you.*

Again, where is this power? *In you as a spirit.* You don't need to figure out what steps and keys you need to perform to get God to release it from Heaven—this life is *in you!* Romans 8:11 is not talking about resurrection from the dead. You don't need life for your mortal body when you die! Do you understand why? Because God is giving you an immortal body after you die! Your mortal body needs life while you are on the earth, and all the medicine you could ever need has been deposited into you as a spirit when you said, "Jesus, I receive You as my Lord and Savior!"

When you were united to Christ, God deposited Himself into you. The life that flows in Him right now has been poured out in abundance in you. So instead of trying to get God to give you healing, you need a revelation of the reality that the healing power you need is in you right now. It's actually been a little mind-boggling to me how we have had revelation of God being in us but thought He left His healing power in Heaven. You can't separate God and His power! You can't separate Him and His life.

How could He be in you and yet all His stuff still be in Heaven? I like to put it like this: when God moved into you, He brought the entire moving truck! Do you realize that's scriptural? Ephesians 1:3 (NKJV) says, "Blessed be the God and Father of our Lord Jesus Christ, who has blessed us with every spiritual blessing in the heavenly places in Christ." Everything Heaven has to offer became ours *in Christ*. Where is Christ? *In you!* Stop asking God to heal you, and start asking God for revelation of the life of God *in you*.

This powerful truth is so simple that we've overlooked it all these years, and yet it's all throughout Scripture. *The power flowed out of Jesus' spirit!* We see the life of God flowing out of Jesus during His earthly ministry. In Mark 5, we find the woman with the issue of blood trying to get to Jesus. Apparently, people had begun to understand that if they could just touch Jesus, they could be healed.

Mark 5:27-30 NKJV

> *When she heard about Jesus, she came behind Him in the crowd and touched His garment. For she said, "If only I may touch His clothes, I shall be made well." Immediately the fountain of her blood was dried up, and she felt in her body that she was healed of the affliction. And Jesus, immediately knowing in Himself that power had gone out of Him, turned around in the crowd and said, "Who touched My clothes?"*

Where did the power come from? It came *out* of Jesus. This life was in Jesus' spirit, and faith pulled it out. The life of God flowed out of Jesus' spirit, through His body, and into the woman! Did you notice Jesus never prayed for God to heal anyone? I dare you to find one time when Jesus prayed for God to open the blind eyes, heal the deaf ears, raise the dead, etc. Jesus *never* prayed for God to give Him the power, to get more anointed, or any of the other religious things many of us do. Jesus understood that the life of God was in His spirit and He could give it away whenever He needed to. Over time, people during Jesus' earthly ministry began to figure this out!

Luke 6:17-19 NKJV

> *And He came down with them and stood on a level place with a crowd of His disciples and a great multitude of people from all Judea and Jerusalem, and from the seacoast of Tyre and Sidon, who came to hear Him and be healed of their diseases, as well as those who were tormented with unclean spirits. And they were healed. And the whole multitude sought to touch Him, for power went out from Him and healed them all.*

Again, where did the power come from? It came *out* of Jesus; this means it had to be *in* Jesus' spirit, and we know that it was because John 1:4 says, "*In Him* was life." The same life that flowed in the Father was the same life that flowed in Jesus.

John 5:26 NKJV

> *For as the Father has life in Himself, so He has granted the Son to have life in Himself.*

Where was the life? *In Him.* The life of God was in Jesus' spirit, and at the moment faith was released, the life of God flowed from Jesus' spirit and out of His body. There was no need for Jesus to pray for God to heal anyone when God had already given Jesus the life to release for healing. This is why it's so important to understand who you are and what you have in Christ. Don't ever judge what you can do by what you can see. When you understand what you have in you as a spirit, you'll never question your ability to stand before sickness, disease, or death.

Don't ever confuse your possession with your situation. Do you understand what I mean? You must know that the life of God you possess in you as a spirit is far greater than any circumstances you are facing. Smith Wigglesworth used to say, "I'm a thousand times bigger on the inside than I am on the outside!"

Every time Jesus laid His hands on someone, the life of God flowed out of His spirit and into the person. Now let me ask you a question. Since the life of God was flowing out of Jesus' body, don't you think it was affecting Jesus' body too? Yes, it certainly was! Did you notice Jesus never was sick on the earth? It wasn't because He was the Son of God; it was because the life of God was flowing continually in His body. Friend, the life of God in your spirit is certainly there to release into other people's bodies, but it is also there for you. Remember, you've got a well of life always flowing in you, ready to release into your body. It truly is the answer for divine health. Smith Wigglesworth said, "It is nothing less than the life of the Lord Himself imparted and flowing into our whole beings, so that our very body is quickened, so that every tissue and every drop of blood and our bones and joints and marrow receive this divine life."

CHAPTER 12

WHO DO YOU THINK YOU ARE?

Hopefully you are seeing the importance of our identity now. Our identity in Christ literally is everything. I pastored for fifteen years before I began the phase of ministry I am in now, and during those years of pastoring, I found the number-one problem for people in the church was not knowing their identity in Christ.

It is such a big deal in life that it has always been satan's number-one target with mankind in his temptations; you can trace this all the way back to the Garden of Eden.

Genesis 3:1-5 NKJV

> *Now the serpent was more cunning than any beast of the field which the Lord God had made. And he said to the woman, "Has God indeed said, 'You shall not eat of every tree of the garden'?" And the woman said to the serpent, "We may eat the fruit of the trees of the garden; but of the fruit of the tree which is in the midst of the garden, God has said, 'You shall not eat it, nor shall you touch it, lest you die.'" Then the serpent said to the woman, "You will not surely die. For God knows that in the day you eat of it your eyes will be opened, and you will be like God, knowing good and evil."*

Satan knew Eve was already made to be like God because God said so in Genesis 1:26 when He said, "Let's make man in our image, according to our likeness." Satan knew Eve's identity, but Eve did not. Notice satan's deceptive statement: "If you eat of the tree, you will be like God." This all came down to identity. Think about it: the very first temptation of mankind was about identity. Eve didn't know who she was and, as a result, she gave away all that she had.

In Luke 4, we find Jesus in the wilderness being tempted by satan. What is interesting to me is that satan brings the same temptation against the last Adam.

Luke 4:1-3 NKJV

> *Then Jesus, being filled with the Holy Spirit, returned from the Jordan and was led by the Spirit into the wilderness, being tempted for forty days by the devil. And in those days He ate nothing, and afterward, when they had ended, He was hungry. And the devil said to Him, "If You are the Son of God, command this stone to become bread."*

Look at the very first temptation of satan toward Jesus: "If you really are the Son of God." What was at the core of satan's temptation? One simple word: *identity.* Thankfully, Jesus knew who He was and, as a result, didn't give away all that He had.

This is why it is so important for us to know our identity in Christ. It is not a catchy religious-sounding statement; it literally is our life.

2 Corinthians 5:17 AMPC

> *Therefore if any person is [ingrafted] in Christ (the Messiah) he is a new creation (a new creature altogether); the old [previous moral and spiritual condition] has passed away. Behold, the fresh and new has come!*

If there has been one scripture of which has become the core of who I am and what I do, it is 2 Corinthians 5:17. If I could claim a scripture as mine, this would be it! It defines me as a believer but also is the foundation for who I am as a person and the purpose I have in this life. When I receive salvation, I literally become a brand-new person. My old way of living is gone—and I'm not talking just about my old sinner lifestyle. When most of the Church talks about becoming a new creation in Christ, it is almost always centered on this one thing: being a better person by not sinning as much. Friend, if that's all that it is, we have problems because I know people of other religions who behave better than a lot of Christians I know! Becoming a new creature in Christ was not about behavior modification; it's about a supernatural lifestyle in which you become free of the curse.

Remember, the life we live on this earth is to match up with the life Jesus has in Heaven. We identify not only with His death and resurrection, but also with His current life. We must understand we are a spirit being doing life in a body.

2 Corinthians 5:16-17 NKJV

> *Therefore, from now on, we regard no one according to the flesh. Even though we have known Christ according to the flesh, yet now we know Him thus no longer. Therefore, if anyone is in Christ, he is a new creation; old things have passed away; behold, all things have become new.*

This body I am in does not tell me who I am as a spirit. My body can certainly tell me my gender, but it can't tell me my identity in Christ. This is why people have a hard time looking at themselves and identifying with Jesus; they are regarding themselves according to the flesh and not according to Christ. You must look past the mirror in your bathroom and look at the mirror of the Word: Jesus!

As Jesus is in Heaven, so are we in this world! Why is that? Because we are righteous.

2 Corinthians 5:21 NKJV

> *For He made Him who knew no sin to be sin for us, that we might become the righteousness of God in Him.*

My identity in Christ includes my position with God and my position in the world. Righteousness certainly is a gift; it is something I couldn't earn. Righteousness is simply the grace of God; however, righteousness is not just a possession—it is my condition. I became the righteousness of God because of my union with Christ. I cannot change who I am; God made me to be righteous.

Don't ever forget that God has forever made you perfect. Because of my union with Christ, I am righteous, complete, perfect, and filled with His life. My identity in Christ is one that is dead to sin and alive unto God because I am right.

1 Peter 2:24 NKJV

> *Who Himself bore our sins in His own body on the tree, that we, having died to sins, might live for righteousness—by whose stripes you were healed.*

Those who quote 1 Peter 2:24 usually only quote that very last phrase: by whose stripes you were healed. To take that one phrase out of its context is to literally remove its actual meaning. This scripture is not really about healing; it's about your identity. Notice that because Jesus bore our sins and we died to sin, it makes us righteous. This is exactly what the apostle Paul was telling us in 2 Corinthians 5:21!

Because we are dead to sin and now righteous, look at what this has done for us: righteousness produces healing. Now before we go any further, let me remind you of God's version of healing. God's version of you being healed is not simply healing you from disease; it is healing you from the source of the disease. Remember that under the old covenant, when God revealed He was their Healer, it was due to the fact that He healed the waters of Marah—not that He healed their body. When the prophet Isaiah said, "and by His stripes, we are healed" it was in the context of Jesus dying to sin, which was the source of the sickness. God's version of healing is healing you from the source, not simply when the problem shows up.

The reason we are told in 1 Peter 2:24 that we are healed is because Jesus made us dead to sin. When you are unplugged from sin, the source of the problem, you are healed from all disease! Righteousness unplugs you. Righteousness makes you so perfect, complete, and right as God that you are completely removed from sin and sickness. *As a result, healing is not just a possession; it is our condition.* Healing is who I am; not something I am trying to get.

Are you seeing yet how important identity is to healing? For the last two centuries, the predominant teaching of healing has been focused on "by whose stripes you were healed" instead of "you are dead to sin so you can live for righteousness." I thank God for all the pioneers of the faith who caught the revelation of healing over the centuries and began to see that healing is the will of God. But we must continue to grow in revelation and understand more than just God's character; we must understand our identity. The moment you understand your identity in Christ, it removes all barriers, all doubt, and all religion.

You can't have divine health without first being righteous. First Peter 2:24 is telling you who you are, not what you need to get! Because of who you are, it shows you what you have. In other words, once you know your position, you can now know your possession, and it changes your perspective and your purpose. You went from being a sinner to being righteous.

Now with that in mind, let's take a look at one of the most well-preached and well-known stories of healing in the Gospels: the woman with the issue of blood. In Mark 5, we find Jesus on the way to Jairus' house when He is stopped by a woman with a serious blood issue. She has been suffering for years with a continuous flow of blood and has lost all hope—until she finds out about Jesus.

Mark 5:25-34 NKJV

> *Now a certain woman had a flow of blood for twelve years, and had suffered many things from many physicians. She had spent all that she had and was no better, but rather grew worse. When she heard about Jesus, she came behind Him in the crowd and touched His garment. For she said, "If only I may touch His clothes, I shall be made well." Immediately the fountain of her blood was dried up, and she felt in her body that she was healed of the affliction. And Jesus, immediately knowing in Himself that power had gone out of Him, turned around in the crowd and said, "Who touched My clothes?" But His disciples said to Him, "You see the multitude thronging You, and You say, 'Who touched Me?'" And He looked around to see her who had done this thing. But the woman, fearing and trembling, knowing what had happened to her, came and fell down before Him and told Him the whole truth. And He said to her, "Daughter, your faith has made you well. Go in peace, and be healed of your affliction."*

In this story, there are basically two characters involved—Jesus and the woman—or you could say a righteous man and a sinner. Remember that everyone Jesus ministered to was a sinner. There was none who were righteous on the earth except for Jesus until salvation was made available for us. Now with that in mind, I have a very important question to ask you. Are you ready?

Here is the question. When you read this story, which person do you identify with: Jesus or the woman with the issue of blood?

Every time I ask this question in a crowd, I get an overwhelming shout of, "The woman with the issue of blood." What is interesting is that all of the people who are responding that they identify with the woman with the blood issue—these people are all Christians. Now most people would have no issue with that response because so many Christians are dealing with sickness. But let me reword the question: When you read this story, which person do you identify with: the righteous person or the sinner? Why would righteous people identify with a sinner? I can tell you exactly why; it is because the Church has an identity crisis.

For centuries, when Christians read the Gospels, they have been taught to identify with the sinners who went to Jesus. Why would preachers teach Christians to identify with the sinner? Because we don't view the woman with the blood issue as a sinner; we view that woman as sick. We look past her identity and look at her situational need.

Let me fill you in on a secret: this story of the woman with the issue of blood is a tremendous story on how the sinner gets healed.

This is not how the righteous person gets healed.

Think on that.

Certainly, there are tremendous faith principles that can be taught and pulled from these stories. There are the truths of going all in, letting go of the world's system, the power of our words, and trust in Jesus—but you cannot use this to teach Christians how to receive what they already have.

Why would we read the Gospels and identify with the sinner instead of with Christ? Because when Christians are sick, they identify with the need instead of the position of righteousness. For centuries and centuries, preachers have taught Christians "by the stripes of Jesus, you were healed" (because they are righteous) and then teach them to identify with the sinner on how to get their healing. When you take a step back and truly think about it, it makes no sense why this would be done.

Why would we look to a sinner to show us how to get what Jesus already got us? When we read the Gospels, we must read them through the lens of redemption in the very same way we would read the old covenant. As a whole, the Church has been taught new covenant realities from the viewpoint of the Gospels—and it doesn't work. The Gospels are a tremendous place for the sons and daughters of God to look at the Son of God and learn how to administer healing, flow in the gifts, and walk in the supernatural. But if you are going to the Gospels to look at all the sinners to learn how to walk in health, you are doing it all wrong.

Friend, this right here is why the Church as a whole is absolutely powerless and struggles to walk in the fullness of Christ: we do not know who we are. *As the body of Christ, we are confessing new-creation realities while viewing ourselves as the sinner—and it just doesn't work.*

Right now the world has gone mad because they can't even figure out if they are a boy or girl. There are people who have even gone past that and are now identifying as animals. As sad as it is, there is even greater madness in the Church. While the Church looks down on the world because they can't figure out if they are a boy or girl, the Church still can't figure out if they are a saint or a sinner.

Within the body of Christ, there has been a statement going around for a long time that says, "I am just a sinner saved by grace." That statement sounds spiritual but it has no truth in it at all—but it does reveal the identity crisis in the Church. When it comes to healing, it gets even worse. Because the same people who would chide Christians for saying they are "just a sinner saved by grace" will still go about as a Christian identifying with the sinner in the stories of Jesus!

Now let's just get down to the issue. Why would a righteous person identify with the woman with the issue of blood or any other person who came to Jesus for healing? It is simple: they see themselves as sick so they identify with the sick person. Why do we as Christians do that? Because we don't feel healed, we change our identity.

Does that sound familiar? "I don't feel like a girl, so I now identify as a boy." Now let's get Christian with it: "I don't feel healed, so I identify as a sinner."

No Christian who has a decent understanding of Bible truths would consciously identify as a sinner, but *isn't it interesting how we allow circumstances to change our identity?*

Is it possible that satan is doing the same thing to the righteous person on the earth that he did with Eve and with Jesus?

Is it possible that satan's go-to temptation for the righteous is to get you to change your identity?

Friend, if you don't know who you are, you will not know what you have; your position determines your possession. Why are Christians identifying with the sinners in the Gospel stories of healing instead of identifying with the Healer? This is why you must grab hold of knowing your union and identification with Christ. You can't be "healed by the stripes of Jesus" without being the righteousness of God in Christ. Righteousness, your position, produces healing, your possession. If you are a righteous person, identify with the righteous One in the story!

What would happen if you switched characters in the story? Instead of seeing yourself as the woman with the issue of blood, what if you saw yourself as Christ, the Healer, the righteous one? If I am in a position in which healing is needed in my body, instead of working on my confession, what if I began to work on my perception?

Every time you read a story in the Gospels of someone coming to Jesus for healing, see yourself as Jesus in that story. Friend, after salvation, I am no longer that sinner trying to get to Jesus to touch His garment. As a new creation in Christ, I stepped into the Healer and He stepped into me. As a result, His healing power now flows in me.

When I was a sinner, I was trying to touch that garment. As a man in Christ, I am now wearing that garment! I now wear that garment of salvation and that robe of righteousness! The dead-raising power of God now flows in me! When I identify with Christ, I am now the righteous one whom sinners are trying to get to—not the other way around.

When you understand your position, you will understand your possession because of a change in perception.

I remember preaching for The House Church in Pauls Valley, Oklahoma, a few years ago. During the Saturday night service, I was preaching on our union with Christ, and then I began to go through the crowd and minister to different people. I laid hands on two different people who were deaf and each time their ears opened up. I worked my way through the crowd as miracles were continuing to happen. When I got to the left side of the auditorium, there was a man sitting in front of a walker who lifted his hand and told me he had multiple sclerosis. Then he said, "While you were on the other side of the auditorium, I felt a heat go all through my body." When I heard that, I said, "Well, you don't need me then. God is already working in you," and then I walked off and we finished off the service.

The next morning, at the end of the service, a man came up to me and introduced himself. His name was Paul, and he had a huge smile on his face. He said, "Do you remember me?" And I said, "No sir, I don't." Paul said, "I'm the guy who had multiple sclerosis. Now look at me!" Paul began to bend and squat, stand on one leg, and show me how all the pain was gone and he had all of his balance and motion back. Paul told me that he had been diagnosed with multiple sclerosis over twenty years ago, and it had gotten so bad he had to stop riding his motorcycle and stop working; before the conference, he could barely walk even with the walker.

He said that when he woke up that morning, his wife had to leave for church early because she was singing on the worship team and so he was unable to ride with her. He still wanted to go to church. So he said, "I got dressed, got into our other car, and drove to church." He said he pulled into the church parking lot and realized he didn't have a cane with him. He called his wife to come help him out of the car, but she didn't answer. He then called one of his friends who was an usher and he didn't answer. So, Paul decided to just get out of the car and try to make it to the front door of the church—but that's when he realized he was healed! He got out of the car and walked into the Sunday morning service. He said it was the first time in years he was able to stand up during the praise and worship and actually get to enjoy it! Paul's testimony blessed me so much. I was standing there with a big smile, but my eyes filled with tears as he looked at me and said, "Chad, I feel like I got my life back. Now imagine what I can get to do now!"

Paul was waiting to get what Jesus already got him, like hundreds and hundreds of millions of Christians all over the world. Paul just needed to stop identifying as someone in need of healing and start identifying as the one who had healing. It is amazing what happens when you stop becoming conscious of you and start becoming conscious of Jesus.

Satan wants you to identify with the sinner so you will give away your healing and work to get what Jesus already got you. Friend, don't allow your circumstances to change your identity. Just because circumstances change, your identity doesn't change. You must see yourself as the branch that is divinely connected to the Vine. You must identify with the One who created you!

Colossians 3:10 NKJV

> And have put on the new man who is renewed in knowledge according to the image of Him who created him.

When you read the Gospels, read it from the viewpoint of the new creature in Christ, one who is in the image of Christ. Again, I am not saying that you are Jesus. There is only one King of Kings and Lord of Lords. There is only one Lamb of God. He stands alone in His position as the Son of God, but you are the branch connected to the Vine—you are the body connected to the Head. We are one spirit with the Lord.

What Jesus did as Savior, none of us can do. But what He did as a righteous man in representing the Father and dominating the curse—we can do. Renew your mind and see yourself according to His image.

We must get our identity right so that we see right; otherwise, you will always be the one running to Jesus instead of the sinner running to you. Why would they run to you? Because they see Jesus in you! But how will they see Jesus in you when you don't even see it yourself?

Colossians 1:27 NKJV

> *To them God willed to make known what are the riches of the glory of this mystery among the Gentiles: which is Christ in you, the hope of glory.*

Galatians 2:20 NKJV

> *I have been crucified with Christ; it is no longer I who live but Christ lives in me; and the life which I now live in the flesh I live by faith in the Son of God, who loved me and gave Himself for me.*

My friend, it is no longer just you anymore. When you got saved, you became a new creation in Christ. Christ lives in you and you live in Him. Don't ever identify with the sinner again. The moment you see yourself as the sinner, you see yourself as lacking, insufficient, and trying to get to Jesus to get what He has. If Jesus has it, you have it. If Jesus can't have it, you can't have it. What Jesus can do, you can do. Change your perception to the right position and it will reveal your possessions and your purpose.

The moment you see yourself as Jesus, you cannot be condemned; you have all of Heaven's resources and you are fully supplied.

CHAPTER 13

RECEIVING YOUR HEALING IS FOR THE SINNER

God's version of "I am your Healer" is that He removed you from the source of sickness. When you died to sin—that is when God healed you.

I hope the title of this chapter grabbed your attention. I was definitely going for the shock factor on it! Why? Because I want to grab your attention and really make you think.

Now let's address the elephant in the room. Am I saying there are not Christians who are sick? No. I am not stupid because obviously there are millions of Christians around the world who are sick or have some type of physical issue. So then yes, they need to see healing take place in their body, and I will deal with this in a later chapter. But there is a vast difference between the Christian and the sinner in the area of healing.

The Christian has the healing power of God within them; the sinner does not. When you see yourself as the sinner, you are needing to receive. When you see yourself as the believer, you simply need to release.

So let me ask you a question. Does 1 Peter 2:24 say that the righteous person is healed? Certainly it does. So let me ask you another question. *How can you receive what you have already been given?*

1 Peter 2:24 NKJV

> *Who Himself bore our sins in His own body on the tree, that we, having died to sins, might live for righteousness—by whose stripes you were healed.*

You see, it's simple questions like this that begin to confound the preachers of our day.

Is 1 Peter 2:24 written to the Christian or the sinner? It is written to the Christian.

Is 1 Peter 2:24 telling you what to receive? Absolutely not.

So why have we turned 1 Peter 2:24 into a job description instead of an identity description?

We preach to people that Jesus has paid the price for your healing and that healing is already yours, and then we tell them to come up to the prayer line so they can receive their healing!

How can it be yours but now you have to come get it?

Do you see what has been going on in our churches? Even the preachers don't believe you have it.

I remember one time, several years ago, I had returned home from preaching at a conference. My son Jake was twelve years old at the time. We were talking about his weekend and then he said, "Hey Dad, I have a question." He said, "This morning at church, the pastor was preaching on healing and was telling everyone over and over in his sermon that Jesus had already provided healing and that by the stripes of Jesus, everyone was already healed. And then he told everyone, 'If you need healing, come up here so you can receive your healing.'" Jake said, "Dad, it doesn't make sense. Why would he tell everyone they were already healed and then tell them to come get their healing?" I couldn't help but laugh, but then be extremely proud of my son. Even at twelve years old, Jake understood that it didn't make sense. How could you get something you already have?

We have acted like Jesus has provided our healing, but it's in a bank and now I have to figure out how to make that withdrawal. Is it right confessions, using my authority, keeping my love walk perfect—like, how many keys and steps are there in the formula to make the withdrawal? Why would that healing power not be in me when I am the temple of God? You mean to tell me that God is in me, but He left the power in Heaven? Are you telling me that Romans 8:11 isn't true when I am told that the same Spirit (who is in me) who raised Jesus from the dead is giving life to my body?

In Christ, we are not receivers; we are releasers. I know it sounds like I am mincing words, but the words we use change our perspective. *If you need to receive something, it is because you do not have it. If you release something, it means you do have it.* We are not trying to receive healing; we are releasers of healing.

To receive something means you don't have it; but in Christ, we have received all Heaven has available.

Ephesians 1:3 NKJV

> *Blessed be the God and Father of our Lord Jesus Christ, who has blessed us with every spiritual blessing in the heavenly places in Christ.*

You won't find the apostle Paul telling you how to receive your healing. Have you ever even noticed that? Show me in Paul's letters to the churches where he ever gives you steps on how to receive your healing. You can look all you want, but you won't find it. Healing is a massive part of redemption and you would think that the apostle Paul, who wrote two thirds of the New Testament, would have at least touched on it—but he didn't. Do you know why? Because Paul understood that our covenant with God not only included healing, but completely disconnected us from disease. Paul understood that in the Kingdom there is no sickness. The apostle Paul was teaching us about Kingdom culture. Why show you how to receive something that you already have?

Now again, I know that there are Christians all over the world who are sick and have physical issues; I am not denying that, but all throughout the New Testament, we never find instructions on how to receive our healing. What we do find Paul telling us to do is to walk in *Who* you have received.

Colossians 2:6 NKJV

> *As you therefore have received Christ Jesus the Lord, so walk in Him.*

If I have received Christ, I have received everything. If I am a branch connected to the Vine, all of Him flows in me. It is in Him that I am to live and move and have my being (Acts 17:28)!

How much of our teaching on healing is teaching the righteous person how to walk in what they have already been given?

Let me fill you in on a secret: the Christian doesn't need to receive their healing; they need to know who they are. Teach people who they are and watch what begins to happen in their lives.

Now I am certainly not against laying hands on Christians and ministering healing to them; however, my preference is for people to see healing take place without my involvement. I want the focus to be on the Christ in them instead of Chad before them; however, we do lay hands on people for healing when necessary. When it comes to healing, it really is simply about the life of God flowing into their body. Whether it's flowing out of me as a spirit or out of them as a spirit, it's simply about the life of God flowing into the body.

You will find that in my services, I don't teach people how to get healed. I've been proving this for quite a while now that if you will simply make people aware of the Christ within them, things begin to happen. I don't want you to focus on you; I want you to focus on Him. The moment I start talking to you about your faith, that's the moment we stop the flow of miracles. Do you know why? Because the moment I start talking about your faith, I turned your eyes on you and off of Jesus. Do you know why I teach people that the healing power of God is already on the inside of them? Because that's what the new covenant teaches! And do you know what happens? People get healed.

For years now, I have dealt with ministers who want to make spiritual excuses for why I see things happen in our services. I am not denying the gifts and callings of God. I know to what office God has placed me in, but I also know what is available to every new creation in Christ. In the end, it's not about a grace or a gift; it is about perspective and hunger. Any hungry believer with the right perspective can experience God.

It's amazing how many people get healed just sitting in a service while I preach on new-creation realities and our union with Christ. I am not teaching believers to receive anything; I am teaching them to be aware of Who they have already received and now walk in it.

While I was preaching at a healing conference in Arkansas, a young boy, who had broken his wrist two days before, got up and went to the bathroom. His mother went with him and took off the soft cast so he could wash his hands. The mother said that while he was washing his hands, he exclaimed, "Mom, it doesn't hurt anymore." The mother said she watched all the swelling and bruising disappear—in the bathroom! He went to the doctor a few days later and the doctors confirmed the wrist was completely healed.

Christians have been taught 1 Peter 2:24 from the standpoint of what they need to receive instead of who they are. We have told the righteous person what they need to get instead of telling them who they are. *Don't ever forget: your position determines your possession.* I am not trying to receive my healing; my identity is that of healed because my identity is that of righteous.

Essentially, most charismatic preachers have been telling righteous people the very same thing the devil has been telling righteous people: do this and you'll get it (even though they already have it).

How do I preach to you for an hour that you already have it and then tell you to come get it? The true gospel of healing is that you have been healed from the source and that healing is a possession of your position in Christ!

"I am the Lord who heals you!" God made this revealing statement to the Israelites in light of healing the source of the problem: the waters of Marah.

"By His stripes, we are healed." Isaiah made this revealing statement in light of what Jesus was going to do in healing us from the source of the problem: sin.

"By whose stripes, you were healed." Peter made this revealing statement to the Church in light of Jesus healing the source of the problem: sin.

Everything that is flowing through Jesus in Heaven is flowing in you now. *You don't need to receive your healing; you need to release your righteousness.* What's the possibility that you don't need to get a possession, but that you need to change your perception by understanding your position? *What's the possibility that the only thing hindering the healing power of God from flowing is that I think I don't have it?*

One time I was preaching at a youth camp in Memphis, Tennessee. I began telling testimonies to these teenagers about some miracles I had seen before and then began a simple teaching about our union with Christ. In that message, I began to tell them they didn't have to have sickness and if they did have anything wrong, healing would flow in their bodies. Do you know what happened?

I had a word of knowledge about someone with scoliosis. I walked over to this teenage boy and placed my hands on his back. He exclaimed, "Something is moving in my back!" He stood up and his back was completely straight! Directly behind him, a young girl was crying and she raised her hand. I asked her what was wrong and she said, "I was walking around the camp this morning and I told God, 'God, I don't know if I really believe in all this stuff about healing. If it is real, I ask You to show me something tonight.'" Look at what

God did for this young girl! But then, do you know what happened? Miracles started breaking out in the auditorium. Without me laying hands or praying for anyone else, teenagers started getting healed all over the room.

There was a young girl who was sitting on the front row and suddenly, the skin disease that was all over her body disappeared. Then a young girl in the back raised her hand and said, "My twisted leg just straightened up!" She was born with a leg that was turned inward and while she was sitting there, she said she watched her leg just start turning to the proper position! Then an adult in the back lifted his hand and said that a growth on his leg had just disappeared. And then it was like popcorn! All these kids started raising their hands and giving testimonies of things that were happening in their bodies. My goodness! Oh the stories I could tell you that have happened in youth camps I have preached at. Kids will just grab hold of it and run with it!

Now, believe me when I say that I totally understand that if you are looking at a physical issue in the mirror or your body is screaming at you, it may seem like you aren't healed. But again, *why would you allow your feelings to change your identity?*

What's the possibility that the only thing that you need to do is simply see that you are dead to sin and thus dead to the symptoms?

What's the possibility that because you are the temple of God and Christ lives so big in you, that it really is impossible to be sick?

What's the possibility it's impossible for you to lose your sight, lose your hearing, have heart disease, for a tumor to stay in your body, or to have arthritis or joint issues?

What's the possibility that who I am in Christ is enough and the light that is in me truly overcomes all darkness?

I am not one far removed from Jesus trying to get to Him. I am one with Him. I am His hands and feet. I am the house of God. I am one with Christ, and He is one with me.

CHAPTER 14

YOU ARE THE BODY OF CHRIST

Have you ever seen a body walking around outside without a head? I certainly never have, and I know you haven't either. The reason is simple: without the head, the body is lifeless. Scripture tells us that Jesus is the head of the Church and we are the body.

1 Corinthians 12:27 NKJV

Now you are the body of Christ, and members individually.

Now I realize that neither you alone nor I alone are the entire body of Christ; the Church as a whole is composed of many individuals. It is reported that there are currently over 2 billion people in the world who proclaim to be Christians; that is a lot of members of the body![1]

If you look at the human body, there are lots of parts. There are big parts and little parts, seen parts and unseen parts; however, all are important and necessary. Regardless of the part's size and function, each part is still receiving of the life that flows in the body as a whole. As it is with the human body, it is with the body of Christ.

No matter what your role or function within the body of Christ, we are still connected to the Head and receiving all of His life.

Ephesians 1:22-23 NKJV

> *And He put all things under His feet, and gave Him to be head over all things to the church, which is His body, the fullness of Him who fills all in all.*

As members of the body of Christ, we all have individual gifts, callings, and graces upon our life to fulfill God's plan and mission on the earth. As a whole, we are the body of Christ. However, when it comes to my individual life, I am His body as well. Wherever I go, I am directly connected to Him and the fullness of Him flows in my life. You need to see that you carry the fullness of Him; wherever you go, the fullness of Him fills all of you.

John 1:16 NKJV

> *And of His fullness we have all received, and grace for grace.*

Notice John 1:16 says, "We have all received His fullness." Friend, you are not lacking; we are full of His life and divinely connected to Him. Everything that flows in Jesus flows in us. This is why we are all told to lay hands on the sick so that they would be healed. Why would we be told to do that and yet not have something to give away? You must be a possessor of His life to give away His life! One reason it is important to vitally know that you are His body is so that wherever you go and in all that you do—you know His life is flowing in you.

I am not praying or singing like others, "Jesus, don't pass me by." I'm not praying for God to show up or the Holy Spirit to fill me up or pour out His power. I am a branch divinely connected to the Vine and receiving the fullness of His life every second of my life.

John 15:5 NKJV

> *I am the vine, you are the branches. He who abides in Me, and I in him, bears much fruit; for without Me you can do nothing.*

John 15:5 TPT

> *I am the sprouting vine and you're my branches. As you live in union with me as your source, fruitfulness will stream from within you—but when you live separated from me you are powerless.*

When you look at a tree, you can definitely see there is more than just a trunk; on a mature tree, you will find many branches. Even though there are many branches on the tree, every single branch is a recipient of the same life flowing all throughout the tree. An individual branch doesn't make up the entire tree, but it does receive the same amount of life. All that flows in the trunk flows to every branch and even the smallest twig. You and I are simply branches but connected to Jesus, we are the tree.

It is vitally important that we see ourselves for who we are and our connection that we have to Christ. How many times have you heard someone say, "We are the hands and feet of Jesus"? What are they referring to? They are talking about the reality that we are the body of Christ—but it's always in the context of doing good things for people. Why is it we only see ourselves as the body of Christ when it comes to humanitarian work but not in supernatural work? *Why are we one with Christ when it comes to doing things that sinners can do, but not one with Christ when it comes to doing things only Christ can do?* Why can I be the hands and feet of Jesus when it comes to handing out water bottles and food but not in handing out healing?

Let's step up our game, friend. Let's advance and move beyond this childish, watered-down Christianity that has been promoted for centuries now. It is time we see ourselves for who we are—the direct extensions of Jesus on the earth. *Jesus didn't come to make a new religion; He came to make a new creation.* Jesus came to make extensions of Himself! If I am His hands and feet, then the supernatural power and life that flows in Him flows in me. I can live in divine health, free of sickness, free of sin, and not only give away a free water bottle, but also give away His life that will cause the dead to be raised, the deaf to hear, the lame to walk, the blind to see, the tumor to dissolve, and the virus to be healed—all while I walk free of everything that the sinner is bound by.

There needs to be a new motto in the Church: no more sickness. We need to treat sickness like we do sin. We don't allow sin in the body, so why do we allow sickness? We have Christians come out all the time saying that we need to get sin out of the Church—and we should—but why not be just as strong in getting sickness out of the Church too? *Why are we not just as bold at confronting sickness as we are sin?* Do you know why? Because we think we have a choice when it comes to sin and we don't have a choice when it comes to sickness. Why do we see Christians stand up and applaud when someone calls out sin and yet not sickness? Why are Christians willing to boldly share social media posts about other Christians making a stand against sin, but cautiously share social media posts when other Christians make a stand against sickness? Friend, we have chosen to be separate from the world in one area but stay conformed to the world in the other area. Why? Because we think sickness is normal and/or we don't have a choice in the matter. *How you view sin should be how you view sickness.*

If we are the body of Christ, and we are, it is time we change our perspective on who we are and what's available to us. Look at Jesus and see yourself. If sickness can't flow in the Head, it can't flow in the body. If cancer can't flow through the Vine, it can't flow through the branch.

Say it with me, "No more sickness in the body!" If it can't be in Jesus' body, it can't be in my body because I am His body!

Note

1. Pew Research Center, "Global Christianity – A Report on the Size and Distribution of the World's Christian Population," December 19, 2011, https://www.pewresearch.org/religion/2011/12/19/global-christianity-exec.

CHAPTER 15

DON'T GET CHEATED

I don't know of anyone that likes to get cheated. Whether it is in sports, business, relationships, finances, or other areas of life, the vast majority of these situations happen unknowingly and against someone's will. Many Christians do not realize it, but you can be cheated spiritually too. In fact, the reason we don't all see the blessings of God in our life is not because they have not been provided, but because as Christians we have been cheated. Sinners don't get cheated out of spiritual things because they own nothing and have no control; spiritually, they are slaves to satan.

As Christians, we get cheated all the time out of spiritual blessings. The Bible tells us in Ephesians 1:3 that we have been blessed with all of the spiritual blessings of Heaven in Christ. This means that all Heaven has to offer is given to us when we become one with Christ. As a result, you aren't lacking. As a righteous person in Christ, all of Heaven is yours—now! *To be righteous is to be right—for all things to be made right in your life.* Remember, you are perfect and complete.

Colossians 2:6-10 NKJV

> *As you therefore have received Christ Jesus the Lord, so walk in Him, rooted and built up in Him and established in the faith, as you have been taught, abounding in it with thanksgiving. Beware lest anyone cheat you through philosophy and empty deceit, according to the tradition of men, according to the basic principles of the world, and not according to Christ. For in Him dwells all the*

fullness of the Godhead bodily; and you are complete in Him, who is the head of all principality and power.

Colossians 2:6-10 TPT

In the same way you received Jesus our Lord and Messiah by faith, continue your journey of faith, progressing further into your union with him! Your spiritual roots go deeply into his life as you are continually infused with strength, encouraged in every way. For you are established in the faith you have absorbed and enriched by your devotion to him! Beware that no one distracts you or intimidates you in their attempt to lead you away from Christ's fullness by pretending to be full of wisdom when they're filled with endless arguments of human logic. For they operate with humanistic and clouded judgments based on the mindset of this world system, and not the anointed truths of the Anointed One. For he is the complete fullness of deity living in human form. And our own completeness is now found in him. We are completely filled with God as Christ's fullness overflows within us. He is the Head of every kingdom and authority in the universe!

Sadly, we see in Colossians 2 that we can be cheated out of what we have received when we receive Christ. How do we get cheated? When our perspective is based on philosophy, men's traditions, and what the world considers normal instead of basing it on who I am in Christ. I love how The Passion Translation puts it: "Beware that no one distracts you or intimidates you in their attempt to lead you away from Christ's fullness." Do not ever forget that Jesus is our standard. Jesus is the standard for what is possible for a man or woman who is filled with God, anointed by God, and one with God. The glorified Christ is the standard for the righteous person on the earth. Anything less than His fullness is taking His sacrifice in vain!

Throughout my life in church, I have met lots of very intelligent people who know lots about the Bible. I have listened to sinners tell me their beliefs about the Bible, I have listened to Christian and non-Christian professors talk about the Bible, and I have listened to countless sermons by preachers talking about the Bible. I realize there are people who are way smarter than me in the world and may know a lot more Scriptures than me, but just because you know a lot of Scriptures and theories doesn't mean you know Christ.

I have listened to preachers give their opinions and beliefs about Christian life, and it's obvious that they have read their Bible with philosophical glasses. They sound smart but are lacking knowledge of God. They are not looking at the Christian life through the filter of Christ; they are looking at the Christian life through the filter of their soul. There are lots of smart Christians out there who like to tell you what they think but have no revelation of the Word for themselves. Whatever your opinions and beliefs may be about the Christian life, they have to be filtered through Christ. Look at Him for who He is at the right hand of God right now; if those opinions and beliefs aren't true for Him, they aren't true for you either!

Another reason we are told that you can be cheated out of spiritual things is due to men's traditions. Just because something has been done for a long period of time, it doesn't mean that it is right. Just because something has been taught for a long period of time, it doesn't mean that it is right either. I have watched people turn traditional practices and traditional teachings into idols. Satan loves to get people into a cycle of doing things that are wrong but appear to be right because most people don't question anything; they simply go with the flow without asking questions. If you do something or teach something long enough, people will just believe it.

I remember one time when we were pastoring our church in Arkansas, this group of people came up to me and told me I was going to hell. I was the pastor! I was very secure in my salvation, but I curiously wanted to know what it was they thought was sending me to hell. Do you know what their reason was? They said it was because I hadn't been water baptized correctly! I couldn't help but laugh and yet be in awe of their ignorance. They told me that in order for me to be saved, I had to be baptized only in the name of Jesus, and it had to be in a water baptismal in a local church. I asked them what scripture they had to base these beliefs on and they couldn't really give me anything. I then asked them, "Does that mean I can't lead anyone to salvation who is in a hospital room, a prison, or on a plane? Do we only tell people about Jesus when we are at church?" Do you know what these goofy people said? They said, "No we should tell people about Jesus but then bring them to church so they can be baptized and saved." I was like, "But what if the person is dying in the hospital and can't come to church to get baptized?" What about those in prison who could never come to church to get baptized? Do we just let them go to hell? They just sat there and looked at me with big eyes.

I remember another time I had a group come up to me about the communion supplies we were using at our church. They told me the wafer we were using wasn't right because it had leaven in it. They had a long tradition of using only unleavened bread and red grape juice. Apparently they were fine with the white grape juice we used but didn't agree with the type of cracker we used. I did think it was odd that they were stuck on using unleavened bread but substituted grape juice for wine like it says Jesus used!

Do you know what I did the next time we took communion during one of our services? I told those who were watching the livestream, "It's time to take communion. If you don't have a fancy wafer and juice like we are using here at the church, go grab some crackers and water out of your kitchen." As you can imagine, they weren't too happy about that—there has always been a little bit of rebel in me! Communion isn't about the specific item you use; it is about your faith and motivation behind what you are doing. But do you see how people can get cheated out of the benefits of things because of philosophy and tradition?

When it comes to the area of healing, this next one is where billions are getting cheated: the basic principles of the world. Unfortunately for most Christians, what is considered normal in the world is considered normal for them. How many Christians do you know who prepare for flu season in the fall? Why do they do that? Because they think getting the flu is normal. Well, that may be normal for the sinner who is connected to death, but it shouldn't be normal for the Christian who is connected to life!

We have even bought into the world's normal when it comes to age and health. Where in the Bible does it say that you have to be sicker and weaker as you get older? All I found in the Bible are examples of people with a covenant with God being old and still strong. One example is that of Moses.

During the entire forty years that Moses was in the wilderness, he was never sick and never feeble. The Bible tells us that on his one hundred and twentieth birthday, God told him to go climb the mountain and die.

Deuteronomy 32:48-52 NKJV

> *Then the Lord spoke to Moses that very same day, saying: "Go up this mountain of the Abarim, Mount Nebo, which is in the land of Moab, across from Jericho; view the land of Canaan, which I give to the children of Israel as a possession; and die on the mountain which you ascend, and be gathered to your people, just as Aaron your brother died on Mount Hor and was gathered to his people; because you trespassed against Me among the children of Israel at the waters of Meribah Kadesh, in the Wilderness of Zin, because you did not hallow Me in the midst of the children of Israel. Yet you shall see the land before you, though you shall not go there, into the land which I am giving to the children of Israel."*

How many people do you know who are one hundred years old and can go climb a mountain? Let's be honest—how many people in their forties and fifties can go climb a mountain? Most people today are so out of shape, they can barely walk up a few flights of steps! You can't climb a mountain if you are sickly and weak. The Bible tells us that Moses, even at one hundred and twenty years, still had all of his strength and his eyesight.

Deuteronomy 34:5-7 NKJV

> *So Moses the servant of the Lord died there in the land of Moab, according to the word of the Lord. And He buried him in a valley in the land of Moab, opposite Beth Peor; but no one knows his grave to this day. Moses was one hundred and twenty years old when he died. His eyes were not dim nor his natural vigor diminished.*

This is one reason we are to stop being conformed to this world's systems, principles, and beliefs—what is normal for people filled with death should not be normal for people filled with life. If Moses, as a sinner and former murderer, could live to one hundred and twenty years old, still have his eyesight and all his strength, and could die without sickness or disease—how much more is available for those of us who are the righteousness of God with a better covenant established upon the blood of Jesus?

We even see with Joshua and Caleb that as they had progressed in age, they still were healthy and had all of their strength as well.

Joshua 14:6-12 NLT

> *A delegation from the tribe of Judah, led by Caleb son of Jephunneh the Kenizzite, came to Joshua at Gilgal. Caleb said to Joshua, "Remember what the Lord said to Moses, the man of God, about you and me when we were at Kadesh-barnea. I was forty years old when Moses, the servant of the Lord, sent me from Kadesh-barnea to explore the land of Canaan. I returned and gave an honest report, but my brothers who went with me frightened the people from entering the Promised Land. For my part, I wholeheartedly followed the Lord my God. So that day Moses solemnly promised me, 'The land of Canaan on which you were just walking will be*

*your grant of land and that of your descendants forever, because
you wholeheartedly followed the Lord my God.'*

*"Now, as you can see, the Lord has kept me alive and well as
he promised for all these forty-five years since Moses made this
promise—even while Israel wandered in the wilderness. Today I
am eighty-five years old. I am as strong now as I was when Moses
sent me on that journey, and I can still travel and fight as well as
I could then. So give me the hill country that the Lord promised me.
You will remember that as scouts we found the descendants of Anak
living there in great, walled towns. But if the Lord is with me, I will
drive them out of the land, just as the Lord said."*

Caleb was eighty-five years old when he told Joshua, "Give me
my mountain! I am just as strong today as I was when I was forty; I
can travel and fight just as well as I could then." How many eighty-
five-year-old men do you know today who would be willing to go to
war on the front lines? This wasn't going to be just a battle against
normal men either; Caleb was going to go up against the giants in
the land!

Friend, these are not just "Bible stories" either; these are accounts
of real people who lived thousands of years ago. They had a lesser
covenant with God; we have a better covenant with God. But what
was the big spiritual difference between the results they saw in their
health and what we see in ours? They actually believed in their covenant. Were there any physical differences between their results
they saw in health and what we see in ours? Absolutely. This is a
completely different subject but I'm going to throw it in here. The
people in Bible days were physically active and they weren't eating
processed food filled with sugar and preservatives—but we will leave
that alone for now.

Let me just throw this in here as well. Revelation is progressive and
revelation is to produce manifestations. If we are constantly growing
in our revelation of divine health, that means that the older we get,
the healthier we should get! It's the complete opposite of the world.

117

Someone with the life of God in them should stand out to someone who is filled with death. The average life of the Christian should be greater than the average life of the sinner!

Listen to me right now: death is not your savior! There are so many Christians today who are looking for death to free them from this world of sickness and disease. No! Death is not your savior; Jesus is your Savior! I once had a man come up to me in church and say, "Well, if I never get sick, how can I die?" Friend, that is the sinner's perspective. Who said you have to die to finally be free of sickness? Who said you have to be sick in order to die? Did God make Moses sick so he could die? Absolutely not. Moses lived out every second of his last forty years healthy and strong and when it was his time to go, he simply took his last breath, stepped out of his body, and left with the angels to take him to Paradise.

We have believed in the world's normal of what old age looks like. We have been cheated; but you will always be cheated if you look to the world for what is normal instead of looking at the glorified Christ as to what is normal.

When you believe in what the world believes in, you will get cheated. If it's normal for the world, it should not be normal for you. If it's normal for Heaven, it should be normal for you.

CHAPTER 16

OUR BELIEF IN SICKNESS

We will always get what we believe for—consciously or unconsciously. We have far too many Christians playing defense in the area of healing instead of being on offense. Do you know why we are on defense? Because almost everyone believes it is possible to be sick as a Christian because we have allowed the world's normal to be our normal. This is why we are to set our mind on the realities of where Christ is in Heaven.

Romans 12:2 PNT

> *Don't let the world around you squeeze you into its own mould, but let God re-mould your minds from within, so that you may prove in practice that the plan of God for you is good, meets all his demands and moves towards the goal of true maturity.*

We have stayed stuck in the world's mold in the area of sickness instead of growing up spiritually into who we are in Christ. The will of God in Heaven is the will of God on earth: divine health. How does that get proven? By us renewing our mind to Heaven's realities so that we can prove the perfect will of God.

Romans 12:2 NKJV

> *And do not be conformed to this world, but be transformed by the renewing of your mind, that you may prove what is that good and acceptable and perfect will of God.*

On the spiritual side of things, I absolutely believe our belief in sickness is what is keeping open the door to sickness in the Church. Now we certainly need to take care of the bodies that God gave us and we are going to deal with that topic at the end of this book. It's an area preachers don't want to touch for fear of offending people, but it is an area that we must start addressing because in many ways, we are killing ourselves. But in the area of our beliefs, we are still living like cursed people even though we are right with God.

Do you know why I know this to be true? Because most of the teaching we hear on healing is "steps to receiving your healing" instead of "It's impossible to get sick!" I understand we have vast numbers of Christians who are sick and need healing in their bodies. So when it comes to healing, we are preaching to the problem—but why not preach the solution? Why is it we preach separate from the world with regard to sin but not separate from the world with regard to sickness? If you can be separate from the source, why not also separate from the byproducts? Do you see what I am getting at?

Why would you prepare for something that isn't possible?

Why would you be afraid of something you can't have?

Think about what is normal for the world in the area of health. They are always preparing to be sick because sickness is "normal" for the world. The world not only expects and prepares for sickness, they also prepare to get old and get sicker; unfortunately, this hellish belief system is in the Church. Do you know how many times I have heard Christians joke about forgetting something and because they are in their forties or fifties, laugh about it, and say, "Well, you know I am getting older and you know how the mind goes!" What kind of demonic talk is that? That's language for the sinner, not the one in Christ. I'll hear Christians joke about being in their fifties and having back and joint issues, laugh about it, and attribute it to being older. Why? *Because you still see yourself as a sinner tied to the curse.*

We have allowed the world's view of health to get into the Christian belief system, and it has affected the way healing is taught in most places. In the minority of churches where healing is taught, the majority teach it from the standpoint of "when you do get sick." We have simply stepped into satan's role of standing beside Eve and saying, "If you will do these things, you will get it (even though you already have it)." Satan has no problem with us pushing the idea that you can get healed, just as he had no problem pushing to Eve that she could be like God. Do you know why? Because even satan knows what you have on the inside of you: the life of God!

Satan knows that as a believer, you are already healed because you are righteous. He also knows that if he can get you working to get what you already have, *you'll let go of what you have because you don't think you have it.* And you will spend all your time "living by faith" trying to receive what Jesus already put in you. This is why you will not find teaching in the New Testament of "standing for your healing" or "waiting on God to manifest my healing." Even though it is believed and taught, it is not in the Bible. So why do we have a history of Christians waiting on God to do something regarding their healing?

Satan is trying to get the believer to believe in sickness and then to get the believer to work to receive their healing. He needs you to let go of what you do have and then work to get what you think you don't have.

Satan put that lie into the Church and we are now preaching it for him—then we wonder why so many people in the Church are sick! The Church is preaching faith and authority from the side of "after you get sick" instead of from the side of, "You can't get sick!" We shouldn't be looking at the world's normal to determine our normal; we should look at Christ's normal to determine our normal!

Our belief in sickness has caused us to immediately let go of the healing provided to us and in which we were made, simply because we don't realize we actually already have it. We quote 1 Peter 2:24 as something we need to obtain instead of something we already have. Why? Because most of us truly still see ourselves as being on the other side of the cross where sickness was still possible and, as a result, we have cheated ourselves.

Colossians 2:8 NKJV

> *Beware lest anyone cheat you through philosophy and empty deceit,*
> *according to the tradition of men, according to the basic principles*
> *of the world, and not according to Christ.*

Think of some of the world's normals with sickness. Have you ever heard of flu season? I don't ever prepare to get the flu. Do you know why? Because Jesus can't get the flu.

If Jesus can't get the flu, I can't get the flu! There is no flu season in Heaven.

I am not scared of getting cancer. Do you know why? Because Jesus can't get cancer and there is no cancer in the Kingdom of God. So that means I can't get cancer because it is not even available in the Kingdom from which I live. My realities are what's real in the throne room of God—not what is real in the earth.

There are so many things the world considers normal that we have just accepted it to be normal for us. And do you know what we do? We see things from an earthly standpoint and try using our authority in Jesus and confessing healing scriptures to try and keep those diseases away. Instead of acting like you can get sick and trying to stand against it, why not take the stance that it's impossible to get sick?

Recently, I saw a church promoting "cancer awareness month." How hellish can you get? Why would we promote a disease? You might as well have "fornication awareness month" or "gluttony awareness month." Well, we know no church is going to talk about gluttony. Too many want their cake and to eat it too—sometimes two or three cakes! The point is, why would we participate in making people aware of a disease and yet not aware of a sin? Why promote the problem and not be willing to promote the source?

It's because we believe the disease is not just possible, but part of life. I refuse to participate in disease awareness months. Why would I promote the curse? Why don't we have healing awareness month or the Blood of Jesus awareness month? Instead of wearing a pink ribbon to promote the devil, why not wear a red ribbon and promote the Blood?

We are so accustomed to the curse that even the mention of it seems weird to people—and I'm talking about Christians! I know that some good-hearted Christians participate in these things because of the loss of a loved one or because of a close friend or relative who is currently going through an issue. I get it that it is out of a heart of love and maybe honor, but it is coming from a cursed mindset. If you are looking for a way to honor a loved one who moved to Heaven because of a disease, there are much better ways to honor them instead of promoting the devil. Autism month. Cancer month. Heart Disease Month. Parkinson's Month. You name the disease, there is a month in which it is being revered, and friend, what you revere, you will fear and what you fear, you will serve. It may be from sympathy, but it is hell that is pushing it.

The more it becomes normal for you, the more it becomes possible for you. Instead of trying to raise money for an organization in which the majority of the funds go to administrative costs, why not spend our time and finances making people aware of what redemption will provide? Why not promote that through Jesus you never have to be sick again—and if you currently have sickness in your body, He will heal you right now!

We are one spirit with the Lord. Why would we believe in sickness anymore? If we are dead to sin, we are dead to disease. If we are dead to the source, we are dead to the byproduct. Friend, we are dead to sickness, so why are we resurrecting it?

Romans 6:6-7 NKJV

> *Knowing this, that our old man was crucified with Him, that the body of sin might be done away with, that we should no longer be slaves of sin. For he who has died has been freed from sin.*

Dead people can't get sick—so why would you think you could? When you died with Christ, you were freed from sickness.

The world has all of their worldly wisdom on all of the things that can go wrong with your body and the ages at which these things happen. They have a list of various exams you need to have at different ages. They have a list of things that you are prone to depending on your gender, race, and ethnicity. Do you know what? I don't care about their list. I have Christians say all the time, "Well Chad, you need to use wisdom." What are most talking about? They want you to use the wisdom of the world—but that wisdom will kill you.

Now certainly, if you have been experiencing health issues and you have been "standing on the Word for your healing" but have had a hard time making that connection, there are some situations in which it is wisdom to go to the doctor and get some help. It's important that we won't play faith. If you need to get some medical help, then get some medical help.

People may think I am against doctors and medicine and that is the furthest thing from the truth. Doctors have saved the lives of many Christians, but modern medicine is not in the divine plan of God either. There are many people whose lives have been saved by going to the doctor, but there are also people who have lost their lives by going to the doctor because the doctor made a mistake.

I have had people come to me before and ask if they should go to the doctor. In most situations, I have said, "Yes." Why? Because if you are thinking you should go to the doctor, that tells me where your faith is at. Most of those people are wanting to go, they are just looking for someone to say it is okay to go without being condemned for it. So I say all of that to say this: if it is life and death and you are having a hard time connecting with the life of God, it is wisdom to go to the doctor and get some possible help. But the "wisdom" of the world that I am cautioning you about is the wisdom that is always searching for something based on their expertise of a cursed world. The wisdom of the world is always searching for the curse and preparing for the curse. Well, what you search for, you will find—guaranteed.

Why would I do that when I am dead to it? I don't operate according to the world's wisdom. The phrase, "You better use wisdom" is killing people. All the times I was stepping out in faith to follow the plan of God for my life, I had people telling me, "You better use wisdom." If I would have followed their wisdom, I wouldn't have seen miracles. I remember ministers telling me during the spread of COVID that I needed to use wisdom. Those same ministers shut down their churches because of "wisdom." While I was still pastoring in the state of Arkansas, I was severely under attack from the local and state government. Despite the governor of Arkansas telling the news reporters he was going to shut my church down, I kept my church open and was inviting people with COVID to come to our church and be healed. Do you know what happened? I actually had leadership of other churches admit to me they wished they would have followed my lead and kept their church open.

Friend, I am not looking to the experts of the world to tell me what is possible in the Kingdom of God. I am not looking at a calendar to tell me when certain parts of my body need to be checked and when I need to start using my authority over potential issues simply because of my age. Why should we look for things to go wrong when God made us righteous so that things stay right?

Righteousness not only affects your position with God, but it also affects your position against the curse in the world. We are so right that the wrongs can't touch us—unless we think they can. In Christ, we are untouchable—unless you think you aren't.

Whatever you think is possible, it's possible, and your faith will latch on to it. Possibilities are the hopes you have in your soul, and whatever has your soul has your faith, and whatever has your faith will produce in your life.

What is the possibility that the only reason Christians are getting sick is because we think it is still possible?

CHAPTER 17

A NEW KINGDOM

We may be in this world, but we must realize we are citizens of the Kingdom of God. In that Kingdom, no sickness or disease exist. Heaven's normal must be our normal.

Colossians 1:13-14 TPT

> *He has rescued us completely from the tyrannical rule of darkness and has translated us into the kingdom realm of his beloved Son. For in the Son all our sins are canceled and we have the release of redemption through his very blood.*

We have such an amazing, over the top, almost too good to be true salvation that put me in the Kingdom and absolutely set me free! So many of us have this demonic idea that Jesus came to the slave market where we were slaves to satan, broke off the chains, and then left us there to get beat up again by the devil. No! Jesus didn't just break off the chains; *Jesus left and brought you with Him.* Jesus completely delivered us and then brought us over into His Kingdom.

Notice in Colossians 1:14 that through redemption, we were completely forgiven of sin. Because of being disconnected from sin, it disconnected us from the byproducts. Being released from sin, it released us from slavery and put us into the Kingdom of God. We're not waiting until we get to Heaven to be in the Kingdom; we are living in it now! As a result, what is Heaven's normal should be our normal on the earth. God's will in Heaven is His will on the earth!

Luke 11:2 NKJV

> *So He said to them, "When you pray, say: Our Father in heaven,*
> *hallowed be Your name. Your kingdom come. Your will be done on*
> *earth as it is in heaven."*

When I look at Heaven, there is no sickness, no disease, and no poverty. There are no addictions, mental illnesses, chronic pains, or depression. If those things do not exist in the Kingdom, why do I think it is still possible for me? We all can't wait to get to Heaven because of how great it will be, but why wait to experience the benefits? If we can have God's will of Heaven on the earth, then what are we waiting for? Why not apply this in the area of healing? Do you know why? Because again, the vast majority of us have not renewed our minds to the Kingdom and we still think sickness is possible. This is why the apostle Paul commanded us to change our worldly perspective to a heavenly perspective.

Colossians 3:1-3 TPT

> *Christ's resurrection is your resurrection too. This is why we are to*
> *yearn for all that is above, for that's where Christ sits enthroned*
> *at the place of all power, honor and authority! Yes, feast on all the*
> *treasures of the heavenly realm and fill your thoughts with heavenly*
> *realities, and not with the distractions of the natural realm. Your*
> *crucifixion with Christ has severed the tie to this life, and now your*
> *true life is hidden away in God in Christ.*

My body may be in the kingdom of this world, but as a spirit being, I am connected to and living from the Kingdom of God. Where the problem comes is when I don't realize that and I still see what's normal for the sinner to be my normal.

Most people think that without getting into an accident, you would need to be sick in order to die. Why would we need sickness in order to die? Why can't we simply live out all of our days in divine health, with all of our strength, mental comprehension, and physical abilities, and when we have finished our course and are satisfied with our life—just take our last breath and leave this body. Did Moses need sickness so he could leave this earth at one hundred and twenty years old?

Deuteronomy 32:48-52 NKJV

> *Then the Lord spoke to Moses that very same day, saying: "Go up this mountain of the Abarim, Mount Nebo, which is in the land of Moab, across from Jericho; view the land of Canaan, which I give to the children of Israel as a possession; and die on the mountain which you ascend, and be gathered to your people, just as Aaron your brother died on Mount Hor and was gathered to his people; because you trespassed against Me among the children of Israel at the waters of Meribah Kadesh, in the Wilderness of Zin, because you did not hallow Me in the midst of the children of Israel. Yet you shall see the land before you, though you shall not go there, into the land which I am giving to the children of Israel."*

God told Moses on his one hundred and twentieth birthday to go up to the mountain and die. Did God give him a progressive cancer? Did God have Moses fall off a cliff? No. Moses went up on top of the mountain, looked out over the Promised Land, and then took his last breath. He stepped out of his body, went into Paradise, and then God Himself buried Moses' body.

The world thinks the older you get, the sicker you get. Why would righteous people believe that? Why would we buy into the lie that its normal to get dementia, arthritis, and other physical issues as you get older? So many Christians are afraid of getting older because they have believed what the world believes about getting older. The world has various milestones of age and illness and those of us who have been delivered from sin and placed into the Kingdom still believe those milestones apply to us.

Do you know what milestones I look for in the Kingdom? All the things I accomplish for God and the experiences I have with Him—not disease and physical breakdown. It's not possible in the Kingdom of God, but it is possible in the kingdom of this world.

Think about the word *cancer*. How many Christians are scared of that? Why would that one word cause anxiety for billions of people, including Christians? Why would you be afraid of what you can't have? We have a lot of righteous people making righteous confessions and yet scared of unrighteous diseases. Listen to me right now: what you fear, you revere. I don't care what confessions are coming out of your mouth; it is not about what comes out of your mouth, but what is in your soul.

Luke 6:45 NKJV

> *A good man out of the good treasure of his heart brings forth good; and an evil man out of the evil treasure of his heart brings forth evil. For out of the abundance of the heart his mouth speaks.*

The word *heart* in Luke 6:45 is literally talking about your soul, thoughts, and imaginations. *In reality, whatever has your imaginations has your faith.* There has been much teaching for decades now about our confession. Our words are powerful and will produce life and death, but we have erred in our teaching because we focused on the byproduct again instead of the source. Instead of focusing on your words, we should have been focusing on the soul. *Change your thinking and you will automatically change your speaking!*

I remember when April and I were at Victory Worship Center in Staunton, Virginia, and saw an incredible miracle take place. There was a young girl who came up and told us she had type 1 diabetes but knew it wasn't normal and wanted it gone. April and I laid our hands on her and told the pancreas it needed to begin to function properly. Why? Because in the Kingdom of God, the pancreas works to perfection. Little did we know that right before she came up to us, she tested her blood sugar and it read 321. If you are not aware, a blood sugar reading of 321 is not only high but dangerously high! But this young girl had such a staunch stance on this, she tested herself before being ministered to. As soon as we got finished ministering to her, she went to the back and tested her blood sugar again. Do you know what it read? It read 121. Her blood sugar levels dropped 200 points in less than a minute! Why? Because in the kingdom of God, our organs work the way God created them to work.

This little girl wasn't moved by the high blood sugar reading. It was amazing seeing the tenacity in her face. There is one surefire way to determine where you are in your faith: what moves your soul. When you hear the word *cancer,* does it move you? Does it move your emotions? Does it invoke fear? If it does, I don't care what your confession is—your confession won't change what you revere, and what you revere, you believe is possible.

Whatever moves your soul will move you into an arena of faith or an arena of fear. I can tell you what kingdom you are living from by simply finding out what moves your soul. The stark reality of the situation is also that what moves you today could possibly not move you an hour from now. There is no staying static in the things of the spirit—we are always moving forward or backward; always hedging more toward the things of God or the things of this world.

What do you think is possible? We are filled with God's life. We are disconnected from sin and thus sickness. People don't get sick in the Kingdom of God. Do you know why? It's not possible. The Kingdom is in you!

Luke 17:21 NKJV

For indeed, the kingdom of God is within you.

The Kingdom of God is filled with light and no darkness. It is filled with health and no sickness. The Kingdom of God is righteousness, peace, and joy in the Holy Spirit. People do not get sick in the Kingdom of light; they get sick in the kingdom of darkness.

We live in the Kingdom of God where sickness does not exist. We may walk through the valley of the shadow of death, but we are the body of Christ, living from another Kingdom while we walk through the kingdom of this world.

SECTION THREE

PERSPECTIVES AND POSSIBILITIES

CHAPTER 18

SUBSTITUTING BRASS FOR GOLD

Before Jesus arose to Heaven to take His seat at God's right hand, He gave the Great Commission to the Church, "Go into the world and preach the gospel." Jesus went on to say that great signs would follow those who believed; one of those signs was laying hands on the sick and them being healed.

Mark 16:15-18 NKJV

> And He said to them, "Go into all the world and preach the gospel to every creature. He who believes and is baptized will be saved; but he who does not believe will be condemned. And these signs will follow those who believe: In My name they will cast out demons; they will speak with new tongues; they will take up serpents; and if they drink anything deadly, it will by no means hurt them; they will lay hands on the sick, and they will recover."

I have a few questions for you. My first question is this: when Jesus was telling the believers to go preach the gospel, who were they to be preaching the gospel to? They were to go preach the gospel to the sinner. My second question is this: who were the believers to be laying hands on for healing? Well, it was still the same people—the sinner.

So this leads me to my third question: why are the vast majority of believers laying hands on other believers for healing instead of sinners?

Throughout the New Testament, we find the topic of the laying on of hands in a few different areas.

1. **Believers laying hands on sinners:**
   a. to release healing
   b. to cast out demons

2. **Believers laying hands on other believers:**
   a. to receive the baptism of the Holy Spirit (Acts 8:18)
   b. to impart a gift (1 Timothy 4:14)
   c. to send them out for ministry (Acts 13:3)
   d. to raise the dead (Acts 20:10)

In looking at this, the only time I could find a believer laying hands on another believer for healing in the New Testament was in Acts 9 when Peter raised Tabitha from the dead and Acts 20 when Paul raised Eutychus from the dead. In Acts 9, Tabitha had gotten sick and died. The disciples found out that Peter was in the area and they called for Peter. Peter went to her house, prayed to the Lord, and then commanded her to come back. In Acts 20, Eutychus, who was a fellow believer, fell out of a window while Paul was preaching. Paul went down, put his arms around him, and raised him from the dead.

Now there is an instance in Acts 9 regarding Ananias and Saul (who would become Paul) that would seem to fall in the category of a believer laying hands on another believer for healing—but it is not. Jesus appeared to Saul in a vision on the road to Damascus. During the vision Saul lost his sight. Many people believe Saul accepted Christ on the road to Damascus, but in fact, Paul himself tells us in Acts 22:16 that he accepted Christ and was filled with the Holy Spirit when he was with Ananias. Jesus had sent Ananias to lay hands on him to receive his sight and be saved. So even in this situation, it was a believer laying hands on a sinner to be healed.

All of the other instances of believers laying hands on people for healing were people who were sinners. When Jesus was on the earth, everyone He laid hands on for healing were sinners because no one was saved. Unless I have missed it, I have found only one time we have any mention in the New Testament about believers laying hands on other believers for healing and that is found in James 5. We are going to talk about this further later in the book, but I do want you to see this.

James 5:14-15 NKJV

> *Is anyone among you sick? Let him call for the elders of the church, and let them pray over him, anointing him with oil in the name of the Lord. And the prayer of faith will save the sick, and the Lord will raise him up. And if he has committed sins, he will be forgiven.*

The Greek word translated *sick* in James 5:14 is not speaking about people with small issues such as a runny nose, fever, or stomachache; this is referring to someone who is in a very bad physical condition. I am not a Greek scholar, but I can read after those who are. One person I highly respect is Rick Renner, and he said the following about this passage in James 4:

> [The] Greek word *astheneo* refers to people who are physically frail or feeble due to some bodily condition. This deteriorated physical condition has rendered them unable to freely move about; hence, they are homebound by this infirmity and unable to come to church to receive prayer for healing.
>
> …James goes on to say that when faith is present, the elders' prayer will "save the sick." The word "save" is the Greek word *sodzo*, which in this verse definitely describes a

physical healing or the restoration of one's health. The word "sick" now switches from *astheneo,* which describes a physical frailty or feebleness, to the Greek word *kamno,* referring to a person who has long suffered from this affliction and is extremely weakened from the effects of this disease.

The next phrase confirms that this is no person with a head cold or minor ailment, for it says that after the oil is applied and the prayer of faith is prayed, "...the Lord shall raise him up...." The word "raise" is the Greek word *egeiro,* which means to raise, but it is also the root from which we get the word resurrection. This lets us know that the sick person is gravely ill, perhaps even close to death at the time of prayer. This would explain the urgency with which this prayer is to be offered.[1]

So when we take a look at the New Testament, we find two instances of a believer laying hands on a dead believer to raise them back to life, and the other is the command of laying hands on people who are gravely ill and can't believe for themselves (James 5). Now I am not saying there were no believers in the Bible days who had gotten sick and a fellow believer had prayed for them; certainly not. We just don't really have any specific examples of it in the New Testament. It actually seems like it was not the norm because of the lack of examples as well as James' question if there happened to be anyone sick in the church.

Is it possible we have sold ourselves short on what is available to us? Is it possible the reason there are so few examples in the New Testament is because it was rare for believers to be sick? Is it possible that is why James asks, "Is there anyone sick in the church?" Absolutely. It is a stark contrast between what we see today versus what we see throughout the New Testament with the early Church.

So here is another question for you: why are we spending so much time laying hands on believers for healing when the Bible from front to back is clear that *the main focus of laying hands on people for healing was for the sinner?*

It is because we have substituted brass for gold.

Brass looks like gold and is used as a substitute for gold all of the time. Brass jewelry will serve the same purpose as gold jewelry, but in the end, everyone would rather have gold than brass. Why? Gold is more durable and it is more valuable and God would much rather you have the best that is available.

Numbers 21:5-9 KJV

> And the people spake against God, and against Moses, Wherefore have ye brought us up out of Egypt to die in the wilderness? for there is no bread, neither is there any water; and our soul loatheth this light bread. And the Lord sent fiery serpents among the people, and they bit the people; and much people of Israel died. Therefore the people came to Moses, and said, We have sinned, for we have spoken against the Lord, and against thee; pray unto the Lord, that he take away the serpents from us. And Moses prayed for the people. And the Lord said unto Moses, Make thee a fiery serpent, and set it upon a pole: and it shall come to pass, that every one that is bitten, when he looketh upon it, shall live. And Moses made a serpent of brass, and put it upon a pole, and it came to pass, that if a serpent had bitten any man, when he beheld the serpent of brass, he lived.

In Numbers 21, we find the Israelites once again complaining against God and Moses. As a result of sin, sickness came. Remember, this was the covenant God made with Israel: don't sin and sickness can't touch you. The Israelites never learned their lesson during the entire forty years in the wilderness. They sinned and serpents came among the people, bit them, and many were dying. So what does God have Moses do? Moses makes a brass serpent and puts it on a pole for everyone to look at. This brass serpent was a type and shadow of Jesus (John 3:14); it is a great representation of what was available under the old covenant versus the new. The old covenant worked but it wasn't the best and it wouldn't take care of the problem. It covered their sin and kept sickness away but it wasn't the best. God didn't want His people to have the brass level healthcare plan;

God wanted His people to have the gold level healthcare plan that removes the possibility of sickness.

Isaiah 60:17 KJV

> *For brass I will bring gold, and for iron I will bring silver, and for wood brass, and for stones iron: I will also make thy officers peace, and thine exactors righteousness.*

In the area of divine healing, we as the Church have substituted brass for gold in taking what God had for the believer and substituting it for what God had for the sinner. Under the old covenant, God provided brass. Brass was for the sinner. It would get the job done, but it wasn't the best nor the most long lasting. Under the new covenant, God provided the gold version of healing for the righteous. It is the most valuable and durable because it is based on the standard of Jesus' blood and gives you His life for eternity.

So how is it possible that we have substituted brass for gold in the area of healing? Righteous people have identified as sinners and thus do not know what they possess.

Because of our union with Christ, we are possessors of the life of God and the sinner is not. We are to release what we have to the person who doesn't have it. The life of God in us is to be released to the sinner. This is why in the Great Commission, we are told to go and lay hands on the sinner (Mark 16:18). This is why the sinners all came to Jesus; they were trying to get to Jesus to simply touch His clothes because power was flowing out of Him.

Luke 6:17-19 NKJV

> *And He came down with them and stood on a level place with a crowd of His disciples and a great multitude of people from all Judea and Jerusalem, and from the seacoast of Tyre and Sidon, who came to hear Him and be healed of their diseases, as well as those*

who were tormented with unclean spirits. And they were healed. And the whole multitude sought to touch Him, for power went out from Him and healed them all.

The bronze plan is the mercy of God. The gold plan is the grace of God. God loves people whether they are saved or not, and He doesn't want anyone sick regardless of their background or religion. This is why He placed His power inside of the believer so we could give it to the world, bring them healing, and show them the goodness of God.

So why do we not see much in the Bible about the believer laying hands on the other believer for healing? First of all, it's not supposed to be normal for a righteous person to be sick; redemption made us dead to it and thus untouchable. Second, our union with Christ filled us with the life of God. Physical issues could come if one doesn't realize they are dead to disease, or if they are not led by the Holy Spirit and get into an accident, or they simply stop taking care of their body. In that instance, why would they need another person to give them something they already have? Why would they need you to release out of yourself, as a spirit being, what is already in them as a spirit being? Why would I tell someone I need five dollars to buy a hamburger when I have five dollars in my pocket? The only reason I would do so is because I don't know I have five dollars in my pocket.

If you are like me, I am always thinking and asking the questions, "How?" and "Why?" because I am on a mission and I am determined to continue advancing. Over the years of being in countless church services and conferences, I noticed something early on that hasn't changed over the last twenty years since this became observable to me. I began to ask myself this question: why are most healing meetings filled with believers and not sinners? What do you think? Well, I found that in most instances, it comes down to these five things:

1. Most believers do not know God's will concerning healing.
2. Most believers do not know they have the life of God in them.

3. Most believers are looking to someone with a special anointing.

4. Most believers think someone else has a closer relationship with God than they do.

5. Preachers have taught believers to have hands laid on them for healing.

Do you know what takes care of all of these issues? Teach people about their union and identification with Christ.

When you identify with Christ, you quickly understand that God's will is healing because if Jesus can't get sick, I'm not supposed to be sick either.

When you identify with Christ, you find out very quickly that through your union with Him, you possess the very same life that flows in the Father Himself.

When you identify with Christ, you realize there is no one with a greater anointing than the Anointed One Himself and, through your union, that same anointing flows in you.

When you identify with Christ, you understand that the same position Jesus has with the Father, you have with the Father.

When you identify with Christ, you don't need another person to give you what Jesus placed in you.

The following statements are truths I meditate on daily; if you want some "healing confessions," here you go:

He is the Vine and I am the branch; as He is, so am I.

He is the head and I am His body. I am one spirit with the Lord.

It's no longer I who lives but Christ who lives in me.

I am bone of His bones and flesh of His flesh.

I live and move and have my being in Him.

He is the fullness of the Godhead and I am complete in Him.

I am the righteousness of God in Christ.

If we would simply focus on those statements, it would take care of the sickness problem. Friend, those statements are all scriptures, and they are not just scriptures, they are my healing scriptures. These are the realities I meditate on every day. They keep my mind healthy and keep me in the flow of healing and health. These are the things that should be taught to believers instead of keeping them dependent on the minister.

You will find that in my healing conferences, my endeavor is not to lay hands on people. We have created a culture in the charismatic, Spirit-filled churches of prayer lines where people come up to the front, have hands quickly laid on them, look for an usher to determine whether to fall or not, and then go to their seat—usually not healed.

Now certainly, I am not opposed to laying hands on Christians for healing. I have done it thousands of times and will continue to do so because ultimately, when it comes to healing, it is simply about getting the life of God into the body. In many cases, there are believers who are doubting their position with God and so they are looking to someone else they think has a greater position. I do not have a greater position with God than any other believer; however, in some instances, I may have a greater fellowship with God and/or understanding of who I am and what I have in Christ. But I do not—let me repeat—I do not want Christians dependent on me or any other minister for healing.

I am endeavoring to disrupt the mindset and outlook of the Church in the area of healing so that we get better results, the God type of results that He intended. I am endeavoring to create a new culture—a culture that is truly found in Christ so that we walk according to the standard of Christ. If you look at the major revivals of the last two centuries, when it comes to healing, it has always been focused on getting to a man or woman of God.

I thank God for the ministry gifts. I thank God for the graces and anointings on people's lives. However, the purpose of the gifts and graces is for the equipping of the saints to manifest God to the sinner.

Ephesians 4:11-13 NKJV

And He Himself gave some to be apostles, some prophets, some evangelists, and some pastors and teachers, for the equipping of the saints for the work of ministry, for the edifying of the body of Christ, till we all come to the unity of the faith and of the knowledge of the Son of God, to a perfect man, to the measure of the stature of the fullness of Christ.

Ephesians 4:11-13 TPT

And he has appointed some with grace to be apostles, and some with grace to be prophets, and some with grace to be evangelists, and some with grace to be pastors, and some with grace to be teachers. And their calling is to nurture and prepare all the holy believers to do their own works of ministry, and as they do this they will enlarge and build up the body of Christ. These grace ministries will function until we all attain oneness into the faith, until we all experience the fullness of what it means to know the Son of God, and finally we become one into a perfect man with the full dimensions of spiritual maturity and fully developed into the abundance of Christ.

Notice that the purpose of the gifts is so that we grow into an understanding of who we are in Christ and get to the place where we manifest the fullness of Him.

Jesus doesn't get sick! So why is the bulk of our teaching on healing about the steps and keys on how to receive your healing? Why don't we get people to see themselves in Christ and as Christ so that the Christ can flow through them unhindered? But how can we have the believer taking healing to their world while we are teaching the believer to come up to the prayer line for healing?

My goal in my services is to get the focus back onto Jesus and off of a man or woman. I know there are many ways for people to experience healing in their bodies, and one of them is through the laying on of hands; however, ultimately, I want us to go up to the highest level possible—abiding in Christ and His life flowing from Him as a spirit and into our body. I don't want the people in their seats focused on themselves, their issue, or me. I want them as conscious and aware of Jesus as they possibly can be in that moment. God had the children of Israel change their focus from their body to the bronze serpent, which was a type and shadow of Jesus becoming the curse for us. So why have the ministers put the focus on the anointing of a man instead of the Anointed One? This is why we have so many people going conference to conference trying to get to someone with a special anointing. In one sense, I get it. When you are desperate for help, you will do whatever you need to do in order to get help. Some people are in such dire situations, they will do whatever is necessary to get help for themselves or their loved ones. I am not being critical of these people at all, but I am being critical of our ministers. The ministry gifts are the ones to blame for the crisis we are in. The ministry gifts have taught Christians that they are the sinner needing to get to the preacher to get their healing. Because of that, I am willing to meet people where they are at, but I am also determined to raise the standard to that of the glorified Christ. In those situations in which people are desperate, hurting, and only have their hope in me, well, that's where we step up and manifest God—and then teach them and turn their eyes to Christ within them.

When I was in my early twenties, right before I went to Bible school, I taught in a middle school. There was one student in my class named Daniel. He was a troubled kid, but a good kid who just needed some love and guidance in life. He and his family needed Jesus. During my time with him, he ended up accepting Christ as a young teenager. Fast-forward about ten years later, I was back in the same town where we had started a church. Daniel and his parents came to one of our services. His parents were now Christians but had never been taught anything about who they were in Christ. Daniel's father had lost all blood flow in his feet and was set to have both feet amputated two days later; needless to say, he was desperate for a miracle. I remember laying hands on those black and blue bandaged feet and commanding them to function once again. All of a sudden, feeling started coming back in his feet! Do you know what happened? A few weeks later, Daniel messaged me and told me that not only did the doctors cancel the surgery, but his dad went back to work as a contractor building houses!

I have devoted my life to this over the last twenty years. I thank God for all of the wonderful miracles that have taken place through the laying on of hands, but again, I am pursuing something even greater. I want people in the Church to take their place in Christ and focus on Him instead of the minister.

Because of the way I have taught on our union with Christ, I have watched people get healed while simply sitting in our conferences and just listening to who they are in Christ. I have so many testimonies I could tell you about, but one in particular stands out to me. I was preaching at a conference in Holland, Michigan, and there was a couple who had come to the services. The husband came up to me at the end of the service and said, "First of all, I want you to know we are Episcopalian. We happened to see you on an episode of Sid Roth's *It's Supernatural!* and were intrigued, so we began to watch your videos on YouTube. We found out you were going to be at this church, so we decided to come." He went on to tell me that he had torn his rotator cuff many years before and had elected to not have surgery on it. As a result, he had lost all movement in his arm.

He said that while I was preaching, his leg started to itch. He reached down to scratch his leg with the injured arm and then lifted his arm up and put it on the backside of the chair. It was then he realized that his shoulder was healed! As he was telling me about his healed shoulder, his wife came bursting through the main doors of the auditorium with tears in her eyes. She said, "Chad, I have to tell you what just happened to me!" She said, "I was diagnosed with cancer six months ago, and I had a large tumor under my jaw. Now look!" The tumor had dissolved while she was standing in the church foyer!

The next morning, the wife came up to me and said, "Chad, I have to tell you what happened this morning. I woke up and realized that the three tumors that were on my back had disappeared too!"

Recently, myself, Jake, and April went to Kenya to minister at the East Africa Faith Conference hosted by Safari Mission. Safari Mission is a tremendous ministry based in Nairobi and founded by my friends Vidar and Cathrine Ligard. Each time I am there, we see some great healings and miracles take place. During one of the services, there were two women who had come up with one leg shorter than the other. The lady sat down, extended her legs, and it was obvious that one leg was about an inch shorter. You may not realize it, but if you have a leg that is even a quarter of an inch shorter, it can start causing back pain over time. Your spine starts to compensate for your hips being out of alignment, and it begins to stretch your back muscles, which eventually causes chronic back pain. This was the case for this woman.

After the woman showed us her leg was shorter, I brought her up on the platform so we could minister to her in front of everyone and so that the cameras could catch her leg growing out. When we sat her down on the chair and she extended her legs, both legs were even! We checked several times and she was already healed before she got to the stage—and we didn't even pray or lay hands on her. She had been experiencing severe back pain nonstop for over twenty years, and it was so sweet to see the beautiful smile on her face as she exclaimed that all the pain was gone!

After she walked down the stage to her chair, a second woman came to me who had a shorter leg as well. This time, I took her straight up to the stage, sat her down, and then she extended her legs to show everyone the leg that was shorter. She then put both feet immediately back on the ground because I wanted to take a moment to explain some things to the congregation. When we lifted her legs up so we could command the short one to grow, do you know what happened? We found out the short one had already grown out!

Friend, these are just three of thousands of examples of Christians who have had their focus turned toward Jesus and off of themselves. I thank God for His mercy in that He has provided multiple ways for people to experience healing in their bodies, but He has a gold-level package for the believer. Jesus didn't save us so we could run to another man to get us what Jesus already got us. Thank God that we can lay hands on other believers when they are struggling to make the connection, but we need to move on to the gold package that is in Christ. We need to move on from brass to gold!

Note

1. Rick Renner, "Is There Any Sick Among You?" https://renner .org/article/is-there-any-sick-among-you.

CHAPTER 19

GENERATIONAL CURSES AND YOUR BLOODLINE

Because of a lack of understanding our union with Christ, it has led to errors in teachings regarding healing; one of these errors is the topic of generational curses and redeeming your bloodline. I have heard it come up time and time again from Christians who say, "I'm really concerned that the sickness I am dealing with is a generational curse that I need to break."

Where do people get this idea? Well, they aren't getting it from the Bible! They are getting it from people trying to sell books and make people dependent on the preacher. It is just another teaching that lowers what redemption and our union with Christ truly is all about. If you teach people about generational curses, it is because you have no clue about your union with Christ.

Friend, you cannot teach new-creation realities and yet teach on generational curses.

The issue of generational curses has no scriptural truth whatsoever for the Christian, but there are tons of teaching videos and books on it. Sadly, they are based on this one scripture found in Exodus.

Exodus 20:5 NKJV

> *You shall not bow down to them nor serve them. For I, the Lord your God, am a jealous God, visiting the iniquity of the fathers upon the children to the third and fourth generations of those who hate Me.*

First of all, notice this is written to the Israelites and is part of the Law of Moses—so this is not written to the Christian. However, just because this was written under the law to the Israelites and not to the believer, it has not stopped people from trying to peddle lies to the believer. So what are believers told to do if their disease is because of a generational curse? Well, they are taught that you need to redeem your bloodline because, according to them, diseases come down through your bloodline.

Can I just be real with you? This makes no sense at all when you look at it from the lens of redemption. Let's just lay out the scriptural facts.

1. When you get born again, God becomes your Father (1 John 4:4).
2. We have been redeemed from the curse of the law (Galatians 3:13).
3. I am in union with Jesus (John 17:20).

These three things alone make it impossible for me to have a generational curse. But let's just focus on one of them: God is my Father. Friend, if God is your Father, what bloodline do you have that needs to be redeemed? How could I have a generational curse when my ancestry is one step away from Him? *It is absolutely impossible to have a generational curse and be in Christ.*

The teaching about the need to redeem your bloodline is from the pit of hell itself. It has no scriptural foundation and is simply designed to make you step outside of your union with Christ, step out of grace, and step back into works. It is basically saying that what Jesus did through redemption isn't enough.

Friend, Jesus redeemed your bloodline when He redeemed you. Jesus' past is now your past, and God the Father is the beginning of your bloodline. Leave the issue of generational curses for the sinner. The sinner absolutely needs to get their bloodline redeemed so that disease stops flowing. How do they do that? They need to get disconnected from the first Adam and connected to the glorified Christ.

When you receive Jesus as your Lord and Savior, you become one with Christ, redeemed, and completely free of the curse. For the Christian, the righteous one, there is no possibility of a generational curse. How could you have a generational curse when God is your Father? The only thing you have running through your bloodline is a generational blessing: *life.*

CHAPTER 20

SATAN ISN'T TRESPASSING ON YOUR BODY

A statement I have often heard when Christians are sick is something along these lines: "Satan is simply trespassing on my body and I'm taking my authority over him." It's a common belief that satan is trespassing on our bodies when sickness and disease come. Well, what does *trespassing* really mean? *Trespassing* simply means to enter someone's property without their permission. So then my question is this, "Is it possible for satan to trespass in your life?" The answer is simple: emphatically no!

Let's go back to the Garden of Eden and look at the very first appearance of satan.

Genesis 3:1-6 NKJV

> *Now the serpent was more cunning than any beast of the field which the Lord God had made. And he said to the woman, "Has God indeed said, 'You shall not eat of every tree of the garden'?" And the woman said to the serpent, "We may eat the fruit of the trees of the garden; but of the fruit of the tree which is in the midst of the garden, God has said, 'You shall not eat it, nor shall you touch it, lest you die.'" Then the serpent said to the woman, "You will not surely die. For God knows that in the day you eat of it your eyes will be opened, and you will be like God, knowing good and evil." So when the woman saw that the tree was good for food, that*

it was pleasant to the eyes, and a tree desirable to make one wise,
she took of its fruit and ate. She also gave to her husband with her,
and he ate.

Anyone that knows me knows that I am very black and white when it comes to the way I see things. I believe in being simple and to the point. So let me ask you: can you please show me where satan trespassed against Eve? Did satan make Eve do anything? Did he make her sin? Did he make her eat of the tree? No. Why? Because he had no authority over her to do anything.

I want you to notice this. Satan had no control over her because Eve was righteous. This temptation took place before sin had entered into the world; as a result, Eve had perfect standing with God and was just like God (Genesis 1:28). Satan could not make Eve do anything; as a result, he had to tempt her.

Because of sin, everyone who was born after Adam and Eve was born into sin and the flow of death. Satan could do whatever he wanted to do to those who did not have a covenant with God. Satan was the master, and the people were his slaves. You see this with sinners and especially those who are demon possessed. Satan isn't tempting them; he just overpowers them and does it. Why? They are slaves to sin.

However, we don't see this happen with the next righteous man in the Bible: Jesus. When Jesus was in the wilderness for forty days, satan came to tempt Jesus.

Matthew 4:1-11 NKJV

Then Jesus was led up by the Spirit into the wilderness to be tempted
by the devil. And when He had fasted forty days and forty nights,
afterward He was hungry. Now when the tempter came to Him, he
said, "If You are the Son of God, command that these stones become
bread." But He answered and said, "It is written, 'Man shall not
live by bread alone, but by every word that proceeds from the mouth

of God.'" Then the devil took Him up into the holy city, set Him on the pinnacle of the temple, and said to Him, "If You are the Son of God, throw Yourself down. For it is written: 'He shall give His angels charge over you,' and 'In their hands they shall bear you up, Lest you dash your foot against a stone.'" Jesus said to him, "It is written again, 'You shall not tempt the Lord your God.'" Again, the devil took Him up on an exceedingly high mountain, and showed Him all the kingdoms of the world and their glory. And he said to Him, "All these things I will give You if You will fall down and worship me." Then Jesus said to him, "Away with you, Satan! For it is written, 'You shall worship the Lord your God, and Him only you shall serve.'" Then the devil left Him, and behold, angels came and ministered to Him.

So, I've got a question for you: where did satan trespass against Jesus? I'll wait.

Oh, that's right. Satan couldn't make Jesus do anything. If satan can just trespass and do whatever he wants without our permission, why didn't he make Jesus turn the rocks into bread? Why didn't satan just push Jesus off the temple? Why didn't satan make Jesus worship him? Let's take it a step further: why didn't satan just kill Jesus right there if he could do whatever he wanted to do? Why didn't satan ever trespass against Jesus' body and make Him sick?

It is still the same answer as it was with Eve: satan cannot trespass against a righteous person. Righteous people are masters over satan; he can't do whatever he wants because he must have our permission.

Now this is where people get religious and say, "Well, that was Jesus." Well, first of all, what about Adam and Eve? Second, if you want to go with the stance that satan couldn't do anything to Jesus because he was Jesus—that works for me. Because when we begin to identify with Jesus, then it puts you in the same position where satan can't do anything to you without your permission too!

This is why satan is referred to in the New Testament as a liar (John 8:44), deceiver (Revelation 12:9), and tempter (Matthew 4:3). All satan can do to the believer is bring thoughts, ideas, and suggestions.

We see this take place with Peter and Annanias and Sapphira.

Acts 5:1-4 NKJV

> *But a certain man named Ananias, with Sapphira his wife, sold a possession. And he kept back part of the proceeds, his wife also being aware of it, and brought a certain part and laid it at the apostles' feet. But Peter said, "Ananias, why has Satan filled your heart to lie to the Holy Spirit and keep back part of the price of the land for yourself? While it remained, was it not your own? And after it was sold, was it not in your own control? Why have you conceived this thing in your heart? You have not lied to men but to God."*

Ananias and Sapphira were Christians, righteous people in union with Christ, and they flat-out lied to people in the church about their giving. Did you notice that satan didn't make them lie? All satan could do was bring those thoughts and ideas and suggestions to them and then let Ananias and Sapphira defeat themselves. Notice Peter said, "Why have you conceived this in your heart?" This word *heart* in the Greek is the word *kardia,* which means "the soul or mind, as it is the fountain and seat of the thoughts, passions, desires, appetites, affections, purposes, endeavors; of the understanding, the faculty and seat of the intelligence" (Strong's #G2588).

Satan brought a temptation, and as it sat there in the imaginations of people, just like with Eve, it turned into manifestations in their body. Why did it affect Eve, Ananias, and Sapphira and not Jesus? They were all righteous. Ananias and Sapphira were the righteousness of God in Christ. Why did they sin and Jesus didn't? It wasn't because satan made them do anything; it was because Jesus made a decision to take those thoughts captive, refuse deception, and counter it with the Word.

How you do sin is how you do sickness. How the source comes is how the byproducts come. Can satan make you sin without your permission? No. Then how can he just make you sick without your permission? If he couldn't do it to Jesus, then he can't do it to you.

So what does satan do? He is a liar, a tempter, and a deceiver. He goes around the earth looking for people who will accept his temptations so he can devour them.

1 Peter 5:6-9 NKJV

> *Therefore humble yourselves under the mighty hand of God, that He may exalt you in due time, casting all your care upon Him, for He cares for you. Be sober, be vigilant; because your adversary the devil walks about like a roaring lion, seeking whom he may devour. Resist him, steadfast in the faith, knowing that the same sufferings are experienced by your brotherhood in the world.*

Satan goes about like a roaring lion seeking whom he can devour. This scripture right here blows holes in people's theology that satan can just trespass without your permission and do whatever he wants. If he could devour anyone, if he could do whatever he wants to whoever he wants, then why doesn't he just do it? If satan could just trespass in your body and make you sick, why doesn't he just kill you instead? It makes no sense at all.

Are you getting tired of my questions yet? Well, here is another one for you! If satan is seeking those he can devour, who are the ones he can devour? Satan can only devour the ones who have cares. This is why you are told to resist him. What are you to resist? Cares. The word *cares* in the Greek is the word *merinma*, which simply means "anxieties or fears" (Strong's #G3308).

God is telling us to cast our fears and anxieties and worries over on Him for He cares for us. It may seem hypocritical that God can care but we can't! But the word *care* in reference to God is the Greek word *melo*, which means "to care about or to be the object of one's affection" (Strong's #G3199).

God doesn't want you to care because His job is to take care of you! But the moment we begin to care is the moment we kick God off the throne of our lives and we take His seat to now become the provider of our lives. This is why we are told to cast our cares upon the Lord. You need to kill your cares. Why? Because if you don't kill your cares, your cares will kill you.

Mark 4:14-19 NKJV

> *The sower sows the word. And these are the ones by the wayside where the word is sown. When they hear, Satan comes immediately and takes away the word that was sown in their hearts. These likewise are the ones sown on stony ground who, when they hear the word, immediately receive it with gladness; and they have no root in themselves, and so endure only for a time. Afterward, when tribulation or persecution arises for the word's sake, immediately they stumble. Now these are the ones sown among thorns; they are the ones who hear the word, and the cares of this world, the deceitfulness of riches, and the desires for other things entering in choke the word, and it becomes unfruitful.*

In the parable of the sower, Jesus explains how people produce fruit in their lives. But as you can see, only a small percentage of people actually grab the Word and produce fruit in their lives. Why is that? One of the major reasons is found in Mark 4:19.

Mark 4:19 AMPC

> *Then the cares and anxieties of the world and distractions of the age, and the pleasure and delight and false glamour and deceitfulness of riches, and the craving and passionate desire for other things creep in and choke and suffocate the Word, and it becomes fruitless.*

We are a people filled with cares. Cares about money, health, children, jobs, etc. In the culture of the world, it seems to be a compassionate thing to have cares, especially about loved ones, but don't let it fool you. The cares of the world are simply a wolf dressed up in sheep's clothing. Cares will control you and cares will kill you if you don't control and kill them. Cares get you focused on the world and not on God. If you are in fear about what your kids may do or may not do—*stop it!* Do you know why? Because that is when you open the door and invite satan into your life to sit in your house, eat cookies and milk, and do whatever he wants to do. And then after satan begins to destroy your life, that is where most Christians say, "I'm not letting satan trespass in my body. I'm using my God-given authority to kick him out." Well, that's great if you decide to use your authority and kick him out. But why not go a step better—*never let him in!* Have you ever hear about "poor old Job"? Well, Job wasn't poor and he wasn't sick either—until he started living with cares.

Job 3:25 NKJV

> *For the thing I greatly feared has come upon me, and what I dreaded has happened to me.*

Friend, what you fear, you revere. Job was living in fear; he was living with cares about his children, and it almost cost Job everything he had, including his life. The cares of Job are what allowed satan to come in and devour his house and family.

Satan wants you to care about what the world is caring about. This is why I always am telling my family and my partners: protect your peace. Satan wants you to let go of your peace and grab hold of cares. If he can get you to care, he got you to defeat yourself.

I want you to see this very clearly: satan cannot trespass in your life. It's not trespassing when he has your permission. Whether it's consciously or unconsciously, we are the ones who open the door to sin and sickness in our lives. If you ever have a question about this, always look to Jesus. Look to your union with Christ to be the filter for who you are, what you have, your relationship with the Father, your relationship to satan, and your authority and ability on the earth. Jesus is our standard for the position and possessions of a man or woman filled and united with God. The only thing satan can do to you is bring thoughts, ideas, and suggestions to your soul. He wants to fill your imaginations with deceptions so that destruction can take place in your life.

CHAPTER 21

WHATEVER HAS YOUR IMAGINATION HAS YOUR FAITH

Throughout the last twenty years, the Holy Spirit has guided me down various roads of my study of divine health. It's actually fascinating as I look back and see how He has built these things in me. Outside of the foundational piece of our union with Christ, this area I want to talk to you about has been the most life-changing and inspiring piece I have come across—and hardly anyone is talking about it: our imagination.

Several years ago, I was led of the Lord to go back and begin studying the subject of spirit, soul, and body. As I did so, I began to quickly see the connection of our soul and body. When I refer to the soul, I am referring to our mind and emotions. A lot of Christians talk about winning souls, but in reality, they mean winning spirits. We are spirit beings. It is us as spirits who are born again, but our soul/mind must be renewed. Our body is simply a follower to whatever our mind is on.

I had been taught this subject when I was in Bible school many years ago, but as I began to look at it from a fresh perspective, I began to see how involved our soul is to the health we experience in our body.

3 John 2 NKJV

> *Beloved, I pray that you may prosper in all things and be in health, just as your soul prospers.*

Notice that 3 John 2 shows there is a direct correlation between your mind and your body. You could say that where your mind goes, your body goes.

Now we have already established that satan cannot make you sin and thus cannot make you sick. He is the tempter and deceiver and his only weapon that he has available is to bring thoughts, ideas, and suggestions with the hope that you will grab hold of them in your imagination. This is how he gets you to sin and this is also how he gets you to get sick.

Genesis 3:1-7 NKJV

> *Now the serpent was more cunning than any beast of the field which the Lord God had made. And he said to the woman, "Has God indeed said, 'You shall not eat of every tree of the garden'?" And the woman said to the serpent, "We may eat the fruit of the trees of the garden; but of the fruit of the tree which is in the midst of the garden, God has said, 'You shall not eat it, nor shall you touch it, lest you die.'" Then the serpent said to the woman, "You will not surely die. For God knows that in the day you eat of it your eyes will be opened, and you will be like God, knowing good and evil." So when the woman saw that the tree was good for food, that it was pleasant to the eyes, and a tree desirable to make one wise, she took of its fruit and ate. She also gave to her husband with her, and he ate. Then the eyes of both of them were opened, and they knew that they were naked; and they sewed fig leaves together and made themselves coverings.*

Again, Eve was righteous so satan couldn't do anything to her; all he could do was bring thoughts, ideas, and suggestions with the hope of changing her imaginations. As he began to give Eve things to think about, instead of Eve casting those thoughts down, she began to meditate on them. As she meditated on them, it changed her perspective on the tree. Your imaginations will eventually lead to manifestations.

Genesis 3:6 NKJV

> *So when the woman saw that the tree was good for food, that it was pleasant to the eyes, and a tree desirable to make one wise, she took of its fruit and ate. She also gave to her husband with her, and he ate.*

Notice it says, "when the woman saw." This was not the first time Eve saw the tree physically; this was the first time she saw it with deceived eyes in her imagination. Satan couldn't make her sin or make her sick. If he wanted her out of the way, how come satan did not just kill her? Why didn't satan put cancer on her? Why didn't satan grab the fruit, put it in her hand, and force her to take a bite? Because satan couldn't just trespass and do what he wanted to a righteous person. His only weapon was a thought.

2 Corinthians 10:4-5 KJV

> *(For the weapons of our warfare are not carnal, but mighty through God to the pulling down of strong holds;) Casting down imaginations, and every high thing that exalteth itself against the knowledge of God, and bringing into captivity every thought to the obedience of Christ.*

If our weapons are not carnal but spiritual and they are for the purpose of casting down imaginations, then what type of weapon do you think satan has? What do you think satan's main endeavor is? Where do you think the real battlefield lies? It is a battle for your imagination.

What Eve saw in her imagination changed her faith and led to manifestations.

Friend, listen to me very closely: whatever has your imagination has your faith.

For years we have thought that as Christians, we had faith problems. We have focused on steps, keys, A-B-Cs, and 1-2-3s to get more faith, but it is not a faith problem; we have an imagination problem. Whatever you think on the most will become your reality. You see, as righteous people in union with Christ, we have the faith of God. Faith is actually one of the fruits of the born-again spirit!

Galatians 5:22-23 KJV

> *But the fruit of the Spirit is love, joy, peace, longsuffering, gentleness, goodness, faith, meekness, temperance: against such there is no law.*

Jesus gave us the tools that we need to get the job done. After all, if mustard-seed faith will move a mountain (Matthew 17:20), it must take a microscopic amount of faith to move a tumor!

Most Christians are not aware of what they have; thus, they are easily deceived in their imaginations. This was the case with Eve; she was deceived (2 Corinthians 11:3) because she didn't know her identity. Satan's deception was, "If you eat of the tree, it will make you like God." It was the great deception because she was already like God, but she didn't know it. As a result, she began to work to get what she already was and lost what she already had.

Let me ask you this question: Is it possible that we as righteous people, the body of Christ, are in the very same position as Eve? Is it possible that satan is telling us, "If you do this, you will get healed," despite the heavenly fact that we are already healed? Satan wants you always working for what you already have. Remember, if satan is telling you something, it's a lie. He is the father of lies, and there is no truth in him (John 8:44).

Is it possible that satan is telling you that you aren't healed because he knows you really are? Is it possible that the reason righteous people are getting sick is because satan is telling you it is possible? He can't just do anything to your body; he needs you to change your imagination and see it possible and then begin to care. When you do, whether you realize it or not, your faith just latched on to it and is now working to produce it. Why? Faith is the evidence of things hoped for.

Worry is simply imagining the curse, and we are great at worrying. I've seen Christians who are professional worriers. They are professionals at allowing their imagination to run wild with the possibilities of the curse, and I have watched many of those become sick, stay sick, and sometimes even die.

If your body would respond to your imaginations on the world's realities, what's the possibility your body would respond to your imaginations on Heaven's realities? Recently I returned from preaching at a conference in Germany. While I was there, I met one of the sweetest couples named Johan and Monique from Belgium. Johan told me he had been listening to my Healing Talks that I do every week on social media and had also read my book *Possessors of Life* in which I talk about the life of God within us. Johan said he had developed a growth on his lower abdomen. He said that he made a decision that he was not going to the doctor about it; instead, he was going to take what I had taught regarding our imagination and do that instead.

Johan said he had been thinking about how the life of God is the light of God and how light is radiation. He said, "I just figured that the light that shines from Jesus is like radiation and it would dissolve the growth on my body." So Johan said he sat in his chair and for one hour and fifteen minutes, he used his imagination to see the life of God in the form of light, radiating from Jesus and radiating into that growth on his body. Johan said when he opened his eyes and looked down, the growth was completely gone.

Our body was designed by God to respond to our imaginations. Remember, your body prospers to the degree your soul prospers. Where the mind goes, so does the body. When you begin to worry, which is simply imagining, your body begins to respond. Your fears trigger your brain to release a hormone called cortisol that leads to your heart rate going up, nausea, shortness of breath, muscle tension, headaches, twitching—and these are just temporal effects! When you become a chronic worrier, the continuation of these things will lead to digestive issues, a suppressed immune system, heart disease, heart attack, and even cancer.[1]

Have you also noticed that the more you begin to worry about a situation, the more it begins to take over your life? I have watched people do crazy things because of fear. Your imagination begins to affect how you see your world and results in how you respond to situations.

I will never forget when I was in the Paris airport in March 2020. COVID-19 was on the warpath throughout Europe and people were in a panic. I was on my way to Nagaland, India, and I had a layover for several hours in the Charles de Gaulle airport. While I was walking through the terminal to my gate, two young men in homemade hazmat suits walked by me. Now get this—they were not airport employees; these were travelers! They had their luggage with them and were going through security with me. I couldn't help but wonder how much fear they were living in as they stood there in there hazmat suits, complete with gloves, booties over their shoes, and a cloth mask underneath their plastic visor that completely encapsulated their head. They were obvious examples of allowing satan to use their imaginations as a prison.

While I was sitting at the gate eating a sandwich, I started noticing all the newscasts on the television screens all around me. Do you know what they were reporting? Fear and death. I looked around and saw everyone with their masks on and hearing all the fears and worries of people. I then saw a boy of around ten years old walk over and grab a door handle. His mother screamed out loud, "Nooooooo!" She ran over to him, pulled out a big bottle of hand sanitizer, pulled

NEVER BE SICK AGAIN

off the top and poured it on top of his head! I am not exaggerating! She didn't just clean his hands with it. She literally anointed him on his head with hand sanitizer and started wiping it all over his body. Fear will make you do stupid things!

I was trying to get my phone out so I could film this, but I was laughing so hard, I could barely control myself. But then as I calmed down, these thoughts started coming to my mind, "You're going to India to do a healing conference; do you really believe you won't get COVID with all this travel? What would happen if you got sick? What if you got it and died while on your trip? After all, you are right in the heart of all of this!"

Suddenly, fear started creeping in. Do you know what I did? I got up and ran to the bathroom! I didn't go to the bathroom for physical reasons; I went for spiritual reasons! I went into a stall, shut the door, and just stood there while I meditated on my union with Christ. I began to imagine Jesus as the trunk and myself as the branch and all of His life flowing through me. I meditated on the verses about being one with Him, being dead to sickness, and being immune to darkness. After a few minutes of getting some soul control and getting my mind back on the realities of Heaven, I walked out bold as a lion, I never had any more of those thoughts, and I never once have gotten COVID, even as I traveled all over the world.

Why wouldn't satan just put COVID on me? Because he couldn't; he had to bring the thoughts. Remember, disease has spiritual roots. Satan needed me to unplug from life and plug into death with my imagination. Why? Because he knows that whatever has my imagination has my faith—and my faith always works!

This is why you find the apostle Paul telling us over and over again that we need to guard our thoughts.

2 Corinthians 10:4-5 KJV

> *(For the weapons of our warfare are not carnal, but mighty through God to the pulling down of strong holds;) Casting down*

imaginations, and every high thing that exalteth itself against the knowledge of God, and bringing into captivity every thought to the obedience of Christ.

What is satan going after? Our soul. Why? Because whatever we are most conscious of will be our current reality. His weapon is simply thoughts. If he can get you to think on it long enough, you will eventually believe it and change your perception of reality.

In the Old Testament, we read about the Israelites as they were about to begin taking the land God had provided for them. Before they went into the land of Canaan, Moses sent twelve spies into the land to spy out the land and bring a report back. Look at what happened!

Numbers 13:32-33 NKJV

And they gave the children of Israel a bad report of the land which they had spied out, saying, "The land through which we have gone as spies is a land that devours its inhabitants, and all the people whom we saw in it are men of great stature. There we saw the giants (the descendants of Anak came from the giants); and we were like grasshoppers in our own sight, and so we were in their sight."

When the twelve spies came back, ten of them reported there were great giants in the land, but notice the last phrase, "We were like grasshoppers in our own sight and so we were in their sight." Did the Israelite spies sit down and interview the giants about their perspective? No! So how did the Israelite spies know what the giants thought? They didn't; they imagined it.

Friend, how you see yourself will determine how you see your world. This is why knowing your identity and union with Christ is so vitally important because it will keep you from being deceived. As a result of the unmaintained imaginations of the ten evil spies, the Israelites ended up wandering the wilderness for forty years. Most of those alive at that time all died and never got to experience the promises of God for them—even though it was literally right in front of them. And do you know what happened to the ten evil spies? They died of disease.

Numbers 14:36-37 NKJV

> *Now the men whom Moses sent to spy out the land, who returned and made all the congregation complain against him by bringing a bad report of the land, those very men who brought the evil report about the land, died by the plague before the Lord.*

Friend, whatever you fear, you revere. Your worries, fears, anxieties, and cares—those become your idols, and when you begin to worship them, you unplug from life and plug into death. The result? The curse you were redeemed from becomes the thing you are enslaved to once again; this why satan goes around looking for people he can get to care. So what do you need to do? Use the imagination that God gave you and use it for good.

Colossians 3:1-3 NKJV

> *If then you were raised with Christ, seek those things which are above, where Christ is, sitting at the right hand of God. Set your mind on things above, not on things on the earth. For you died, and your life is hidden with Christ in God.*

Why would we be told to set our mind on the realities of Heaven? Because satan wants you to remain conformed to the realities of this world and what the world calls normal. When we were born into this world, we were raised with what the world calls normal; however, when we are born again and united to Christ, we now have an alternate reality we can live in. But how can we live in the reality of Heaven? We have to change our thinking. We have to change our imaginations so we can change our perspective and change our life. If you don't, you will get cheated out of what Jesus provided.

Our soul is the valve that determines what flows not only into our bodies, but also into our lives. We are now holding the power cord and determining whether we stay plugged into life or plugged into death, and what we do with our imaginations determines the flow. I am a spirit, filled with the life of God, but no life will flow in my body if my soul is connected to the things of the world. Whatever has my imagination has my faith, and whatever has my faith will be produced in my life.

In the Spirit-filled churches, for decades now, there has been a tremendous focus on our words and the power they carry. Friend, let me tell you right now, there is power in our words and what we speak will produce life or death. However, when it came to the teaching on our confessions, we missed the mark.

Luke 6:45 NKJV

> *A good man out of the good treasure of his heart brings forth good; and an evil man out of the evil treasure of his heart brings forth evil. For out of the abundance of the heart his mouth speaks.*

Jesus does mention the importance of our words here, but words are not the focus; the focus is on our imaginations. The word *heart* is again the Greek word *kardia*, which is referring to our thoughts, passions, and desires. Your words are important, but what is more important are your imaginations. Why? Because your imaginations will produce your words. Friend, just as with healing, we put the cart before the horse once again when it comes to our words. Satan has no problem with you working on your confession if you aren't working on your imagination. He will help you sit down and even write the confession sheets with you! Because it doesn't matter what you say if you don't believe it! I can tell you why we have an abundance of knowledge over the years and yet little results. Do you want to know why? We have focused on the byproducts instead of the source—in many areas.

When it comes to healing, we focused on sickness instead of righteousness. When it comes to authority, we focused on words instead of our imagination. Think about it! If your words produce life or death, but those words come from the abundance of your imaginations, why haven't we focused on our imaginations? Why are there thousands of books and teaching series available about the power of our words and maybe a handful of teachings on the imagination? Because satan has no problem with you focusing on the byproduct when you are not focused on the source.

In dealing with people over the last twenty-five years, I have encountered people who know lots of Scripture, have been to church a long time, and know all the right things to say; however, get them talking long enough and the truth will come out—what is truly in their imaginations will eventually come out. Once they stop trying to choose their words, then I get to find out what they have been spending all their time thinking about—and that's usually where the emotions come.

You see, I can tell many times where people's imaginations are by their emotions. I've learned to look past the put-on confessions and look at their emotions. Do you know why? Your emotions are part of your soul. Your emotions are tied to your imaginations. I've watched people mechanically give me positive confessions about their situation and yet I can see the fear and cares of the world in their face and emotions. Your emotions are a very good indicator of your imaginations.

Your body goes where your soul goes. If you want a healthy body, it starts with a healthy soul. This is why John said in 3 John 2, "Beloved I wish above all things that you would prosper and be in health, even as your soul prospers." Prosperity in any area of your life always begins with your soul.

You have to protect your mind. You have to protect your imaginations. God gave you an imagination to produce things in the spirit.

Your imagination is a good thing because it is a God thing—but satan has hijacked it. In the church world, we have accepted the bad of the imagination in regard to the curse but thrown it off to the side when it comes to the good—even though it is all throughout the Bible! Why do you think God was always telling people to meditate on the Word? Meditation is a God thing that the devil hijacked and emphasized in eastern religions. And because church folk don't really study their Bibles, we decided that meditation was a bad thing because of how it is used in eastern religions and the occult. No! Just because satan takes something of God's and warps it, it doesn't mean it is now bad. Most Christians do not realize it, but meditation isn't just a Christian thing—it is a spiritual thing. Meditation is a spiritual principle that any person can tap into because whether you are saved or not, we are all spirit beings.

Our imagination can be used for good and for bad. Let me tell you a personal story. While I was still pastoring in Arkansas, at one point we were in the middle of a building program. We had bought a 19,000-square-foot building that was a former fitness center. During the middle of the renovations, the general contractor called me and said, "Hey, I don't know how to tell you this, but we're going to need another $500,000 because the fire marshal changed the plans for the sprinkler system and it's going to change a lot of other things we need to do." Well, we didn't have another $500,000, and on top of that, he needed it in two months!

I have always been pretty good about maintaining my thought life, but in this instance, I lost it. I had already been under a great amount of stress with other things going on at the church and I just got weak and caved. For the next few days, I was a nervous wreck. Do you know why? Because I had signed on the dotted line stating the general contractor could go ahead and proceed with the work and I was guaranteeing we would have the additional funds at the end of the two months. All I could think about for days was that I was going to lose the church, lose my family, and go to jail!

One night as I was in the shower, my body had broken out in hives and then my throat started to swell shut. I don't like going to doctors, but in the end, my wife won the argument and we headed to the emergency room at 11:50 pm. It was about a twenty-minute drive to the hospital. As we were driving, I was struggling to breathe but I was also getting mad at myself. Do you know why? Because I realized I had allowed my imagination to run wild for several days and it was my fault I was in this predicament. I had allowed the cares of the world to bring cares in my body! When we got to the hospital, I said, "Give me ten minutes to practice what I preach." So I turned on some instrumental piano music, closed my eyes, and began to switch my imaginations from the curse to the Blessing. I began to use the image Jesus gave us of the vine and the branches. I saw Jesus and me connected. I saw the life of Jesus flowing into my body. I kept using my imagination and just focusing on seeing Him and becoming conscious of Him. Somewhere before that ten minutes was up, suddenly, my throat opened up and I was able to take a big breath of air. I looked down and all of that mess was gone from my skin. I was completely healed! And do you know what we did? We turned around and went straight back home. Friend, whatever has your imagination has your faith, and whatever has your faith—it will be produced in your life.

Use what God gave you and use it for good. We use our imaginations to stay connected and maintain our consciousness of God. A God-imagination produces God-fruit!

John 15:5 TPT

> *I am the sprouting vine and you're my branches. As you live in union with me as your source, fruitfulness will stream from within you—but when you live separated from me you are powerless.*

Do you know how you abide? You stay there with your imagination. You allow yourself to stay in a place of consciousness and awareness of Him divinely connected to you. That is our one job: stay connected to the source of all life. Through redemption, we are eternally connected to Him as spirit beings; we are one spirit with the Lord. However, if we want to see fruit in our lives, we have to maintain the connection and the flow of our soul. We need soul control!

Don't allow satan to destroy you with what God gave you! Guard your imagination. Use your imagination to walk in the things of God, grow in your fellowship with God, and stay connected to the life of God. Whatever has your imagination has your faith.

Keep your imaginations on this simple but vital truth: I am dead to disease. I will not allow my imagination to see myself getting sick. I will not use my imagination to cheat myself out of what Jesus has done for me, in me, and all He is endeavoring to do through me. Even in the midst of a pandemic, even though one thousand fall at one side and ten thousand at another, I will not fear and allow my imagination to see myself falling with them. I will guard my imagination and see life's circumstances through the alternate reality of Heaven—I see myself growing older and fulfilling the plan of God for my life free of sickness and disease, with all of my mental faculties and my strength continually being renewed like the eagle's—because I am one with Christ and His life flows through me.

In the area of healing, keep your imagination on the reality that you are untouchable and are led by the Holy Spirit—you will never be sick another day in your life.

Note

1. "Stress symptoms: Effects on your body and behavior," Mayo Clinic, August 10, 2023, https://www.mayoclinic.org/healthy-lifestyle/stress-management/in-depth/stress-symptoms/art-20050987.

CHAPTER 22

STAY CONNECTED TO THE SOURCE

Most Christians who have an understanding of faith, our authority in Christ, and confession are trying to make something happen—but you were never meant to heal yourself. Certainly, if something has attached itself to your body, we are to take authority over it, but all that we do is to stem from our union to Christ. Remember, grace provided the cure. Grace put the medicine inside you as a spirit. Grace will do the work; you simply need to be aware of what you have. It is not your job to work for what Jesus provided.

John 15:5 TPT

> *I am the sprouting vine and you're my branches. As you live in union with me as your source, fruitfulness will stream from within you—but when you live separated from me you are powerless.*

Jesus said, "Without Me, you can do nothing and you are powerless." We have been trying to heal ourselves by making enough confessions, reading enough chapters in our Bible, and doing all sorts of good things. These are things we should be doing to maintain our fellowship with God and grow in spiritual things, but these things will not get you what grace provided. Don't make the mistake of working for your healing. We have a dire problem right now in the Church of people calling their works "faith" and yet frustrated because it's not working! They are working at Faith Incorporated but not getting a paycheck! Your only job is to stay connected and this has everything to do with your mind. Grace united you with Christ so that everything that flows in Him can flow in you.

Do you see the connection? If you have received Jesus as your Savior, you have been united, but there is the whole piece of abiding that must be dealt with. The word *abide* is the Greek word *meno*, which means "to habitually abide or stay put." It describes a decision from which the one abiding will not budge or move from his spot. Jesus was saying in essence, "If you habitually reside in Me, refusing to budge and never moving out of Me, you will bear much fruit." The word *meno* describes someone who is making the decision, "This is my spot; I will not move!" Paul exhorted us to resolve that, regardless of what was happening around us, we would not change our position where the Word and the will of God were concerned.

Understand that your position in Christ will never change. Your relationship with Him is static, but your fellowship is very fluid. We are always increasing or decreasing in our awareness of Him with us and in us. There are many people who started out strong in faith because they started out strong in fellowship. As time went on, the fellowship decreased and, eventually, so did their results. Abiding in Christ is about your fellowship and awareness of Him. It is in that place that growth and victory take place. It's exactly what God was talking about in Psalm 91 when He said, "Whoever dwells in the shelter of the Most High will rest in the shadow of the Almighty." God then goes on to talk about all the results one will see when they make His presence their dwelling place.

When I was growing up, there was a lot of talk of people being backslidden; this was always in reference to someone who sinned and had stopped walking with the Lord. In all reality, backsliding doesn't start with the sin; backsliding starts with being less aware of God right now than you were five minutes ago. If you are less aware of God today than you were yesterday, you have slid backward. You know as well as I do that you can walk into a church service, experience the tangible presence of God, and then an hour later, you can be sitting in a restaurant and God not be as real. It is not because God left you; it's because your mind left Him. God connected us to Christ; it is our responsibility to make that union our dwelling place and keep our soul connected to Him.

There are three main ways we can stay connected to the Source of life. Number one, we need to spend time in the Word of God hearing from God. Remember, Jesus said, "My words are spirit and they are life!" Maintaining the connection really is all about fellowship. When we spend time in the written Word, it puts us in a position to hear the spoken Word. This is why Romans 10:17 (NKJV) says, "Faith comes by hearing, and hearing by the word of God."

Faith doesn't come by reading a lot of scriptures or hearing a lot of sermons; faith comes by hearing from God. In Romans 10:17, the phrase "word of God" is not referring to the written Word; the word *word* used is the Greek word *rhema,* which means "the spoken word of God." If you will read and study with the intent of hearing, the Holy Spirit will always reveal things to you. Friend, the Bible was not meant to just give you information; sadly, that's where most Christians are. Faith doesn't come by hearing and hearing and hearing and hearing more scriptures and sermons; it comes from fellowship and hearing from Him. The fact that the word *rhema* is used reveals that faith flows from fellowship; it comes from the spoken word of God. If you don't watch it, you can even turn reading your Bible into a job trying to read enough scriptures so you can get enough faith.

Just because you know scriptures doesn't mean you know God. Even Jesus dealt with the Pharisees about this very thing. Jesus said, "You search the Scriptures for in them you think is eternal life; I am life!" Daniel 11:32 says, "Those that know their God will be strong and do great exploits." This is not knowing facts about God; this is talking about a legit relationship and fellowship with God. In Philippians 3, the apostle Paul said, "My aim in life is to know Him and the power of His resurrection." Many Christians today want the power without the fellowship—but it will never happen that way. We have been focused on the wrong thing; we are focusing on the power, but if you will simply increase your awareness and fellowship with Him, the flow of divine life and power will be a natural byproduct. So in your study time, don't focus on reading; focus on hearing. I know I just said this but it bears repeating—just because you know Scriptures doesn't mean you know God.

Number two, we must spend time praying in the Spirit. As we pray in the Spirit, we are literally working together with Him. It is one way that we become co-laborers; He is giving us the words, and we are speaking them out. It's impossible for us to not be aware of Him when we are listening to Him and working together. I've found that in the times my awareness of Him isn't where it should be—I haven't been spending the time praying in the Spirit like I need to be. *When my communion decreases, it affects my fellowship and thus affects manifestations.* When I am preparing for a healing conference, I will usually take two to three days before the meetings to fast and spend extra time praying in the Spirit. I do this to increase my awareness of Him and thus increase my sensitivity to His voice.

I must increase my consciousness of God inside me so that I am full of faith in what I have and sensitive in hearing His voice to release that divine life. I've noticed that as I do these things, it also affects the way I see myself. It keeps my mind on who I really am, and as a result, it leads to greater results in the area of healing.

Doing number one and two will produce number three: encounters with God. The purpose of the Bible and praying in the Spirit was to not only give us information and revelation, but ultimately to lead us into encounters with God. God created us for encounters. God intended for us to hear from Him, see from Him, and experience Him.

John 14:19-21 TPT

> *Soon I will leave this world and they will see me no longer, but you will see me, because I will live again, and you will come alive too. So when that day comes, you will know that I am living in the Father and that you are one with me, for I will be living in you. Those who truly love me are those who obey my commands. Whoever passionately loves me will be passionately loved by my Father. And I will passionately love him in return and will reveal myself to him."*

Jesus said that on the day of salvation, we have the opportunity to have encounters with Him; Jesus said He would manifest Himself to us! Do you think that if you are regularly having encounters with Jesus you would ever have any problems with sickness or disease? It would be impossible! When Moses was hanging out with God, the radiation of God was flowing into his skin! When Jesus was hanging out with God, the life of God was flowing out of His spirit into His body! Friend, all the treatments of chemo and radiation can't do what one encounter with God can do!

When you have an encounter with God, don't think it is a one and done deal; *every encounter with God is an invitation for another one!* The more aware you are of Him, the more He will flow out of you. Instead of focusing on getting healed, why don't you just focus on His presence! If He is our Source, then He alone should be our focus. When your eyes are on the sickness, your eyes are not on Him. *What you are most aware of is what you will experience.*

Matthew 6:6 MSG

> *Here is what I want you to do: Find a quiet, secluded place so you won't be tempted to role-play before God. Just be there as simply and honestly as you can manage. The focus will shift from you to God and you will begin to sense His grace.*

Notice that in the ministry of Jesus, He never made much mention of the problem. Jesus never really talked about the sickness or issue at hand. Why? Because He was so aware of God, the problem wasn't much of an issue. His focus was not on the death; it was on the divine life that was in Him and the source of that life. Even when dealing with the sick, most of the time Jesus just responded to them like there was no physical issue!

There is an interesting passage of Scripture in Acts where we see Peter take his cue from Jesus properly fixing his focus. Peter raised a woman from the dead but his focus was not on the dead body.

Acts 9:39-41 NKJV

> *Then Peter arose and went with them. When he had come, they brought him to the upper room. And all the widows stood by him weeping, showing the tunics and garments which Dorcas had made while she was with them. But Peter put them all out, and knelt down and prayed. And turning to the body he said, "Tabitha, arise." And she opened her eyes, and when she saw Peter she sat up. Then he gave her his hand and lifted her up; and when he had called the saints and widows, he presented her alive.*

Notice in verse 40, it says Peter knelt down and prayed. He then turned to the body and said, "Tabitha, arise."

Do you see where Peter put his attention and focus? Peter didn't just walk in there and start making declarations. Peter first got his attentions and affections onto God. He increased his consciousness of God and I believe got direction from God. After all of this, he turned to the body. This blatantly tells me Peter wasn't looking at the dead body the entire time he was in the room. Death was not his focus; life was his focus. After praying, immediately he turned around to face the body and released divine life with a command of life. We know what happens when life is released on death—death always bows down and gives way.

2 Corinthians 4:10-13, 17-18 NKJV

> *Always carrying about in the body the dying of the Lord Jesus,
> that the life of Jesus also may be manifested in our body. For we
> who live are always delivered to death for Jesus' sake, that the
> life of Jesus also may be manifested in our mortal flesh. So then
> death is working in us, but life in you. And since we have the
> same spirit of faith, according to what is written, "I believed and
> therefore I spoke," we also believe and therefore speak. ...For our
> light affliction, which is but for a moment, is working for us a far
> more exceeding and eternal weight of glory, while we do not look at
> the things which are seen, but at the things which are not seen. For
> the things which are seen are temporary, but the things which are
> not seen are eternal.*

We aren't to be focused on the things that are seen with our physical eyes. We are to be focused on the life of God within us. What is real to us is what we believe and will be the confession that flows out of our mouth. You cannot be focused on the results of the curse; you must be focused on the results of the Blessing. Your union of your spirit with Christ must be greater! You can't release life when the death you face is greater in your mind; however, if you walk out of an encounter with God, you will be fully aware of that life and ready to blow away death.

Here is your formula for success:

- Spend time in the Word.
- Spend time in prayer.
- Have encounters with God.
- Repeat.

Make this your lifestyle. Don't make the mistake of those in the past who gained information but never had fellowship. There is no such thing as operating in the faith of God without it flowing out of a fellowship with God. You can know all the keys, steps, and formulas, but without fellowship, you will produce nothing. If you make His presence your permanent dwelling place, you will produce much fruit. Make this your lifestyle and you will experience a life of divine health for yourself and miracles for others.

CHAPTER 23

WHEN CHRISTIANS ARE SICK

So with all this talk about us being untouchable, we can't ignore the fact that there are hundreds of millions of Christians all around the world who are sick. So how can Jesus make us dead to sickness and we still get sick? Because we make ourselves alive to sickness. How is this possible?

1. We think it's possible to be sick.
2. We don't control our imaginations.
3. We don't take care of the bodies God gave us.

Let's deal with the first one. Because Jesus has made us free from sin and unplugged us from the first Adam and now we are plugged into Him, it's no longer possible to be sick unless we still think it is possible. We have to do some considering in our imagination and change our perspective of life. We must see ourselves as dead to disease—that it is no longer possible to be sick another day in my life. Remember: if we are dead to sin, which is the source, we are dead to the byproducts, which include sickness.

Romans 6:10-11 NKJV

> *For the death that He died, He died to sin* [sickness] *once for all; but the life that He lives, He lives to God. Likewise you also, reckon*

yourselves to be dead indeed to sin [sickness], *but alive to God in Christ Jesus our Lord.*

If I am dead to sin/sickness, why would I need to consider myself dead to it? Because everything in this world is telling you that you are still alive to it. Whatever my soul is connected to is what will flow through me. Jesus set me free from the curse but I choose with my soul what I plug into: life or death. This is where I need to daily consider that it is no longer possible for me to be sick. No matter how bad the pandemic is, no matter what the reports may be on the news—I am untouchable. I must properly discern the Lord's body and see myself for who He is.

1 Corinthians 11:27-29 NKJV

> *Therefore whoever eats this bread or drinks this cup of the Lord in an unworthy manner will be guilty of the body and blood of the Lord. But let a man examine himself, and so let him eat of the bread and drink of the cup. For he who eats and drinks in an unworthy manner eats and drinks judgment to himself, not discerning the Lord's body.*

The word *discerning* in the Greek means "to separate, prefer, or make a distinction" (Strong's #G1252). Remember, we identify with His death, His resurrection, and His life. In order for me to identify with His resurrection and His life, I must identify first with His death. I must make a distinction that there was something special that happened here—that I am in union with that death. The death Jesus died is the death I died. Jesus' past is my past.

I don't take communion from the standpoint of just another ritual. When I take communion, it is a stark and solemn reminder that I am eating and drinking to His death, my death, His life, and my life. I am nothing without Him, and I thank Him for everything. I believe it is unworthy to partake of communion and see myself separate from Him. Jesus died so I could be one with Him. I think it is unworthy to partake of communion, partake of His blood and body, and still see it possible for me to stay connected to sin and sickness. I must discern His body in Heaven; that body is free of sickness and disease and yet also shows the holes in His wrists and feet revealing forever the sacrifice He made to eternally set me from sin. When I see myself separate from Christ, that is when condemnation sets in.

Romans 8:1-2 TPT

> *So now the case is closed. There remains no accusing voice of condemnation against those who are joined in life-union with Jesus, the Anointed One. For the "law" of the Spirit of life flowing through the anointing of Jesus has liberated us from the "law" of sin and death.*

We view condemnation as only relating to sin; condemnation is more than that. Condemnation also relates to sickness. The moment I see it possible for me to be sick, that is condemnation telling me I am not righteous enough. How could I be filled with the life of God and yet think I could get sick? Because condemnation tells me I don't have enough life. Condemnation will tell you when you lay hands on someone that you aren't anointed enough. Condemnation will tell you that cancer is a big deal and you should be concerned. The moment you see yourself outside of your union with Christ is where condemnation comes in, and if not dealt with, condemnation will kill you.

The world's normal is not my normal. What is normal for a fifty-year-old man filled with the devil will not be normal for me at fifty because I am filled with God. What is normal for a man at seventy years old connected to death will not be normal for me at seventy because I am filled with God's life. The only time these things will be possible is if I think they're possible—and this is the area that satan is working overtime in when it comes to your life.

Don't you be scared of dying young. Remember, what you fear is what you revere and what you revere, you will be a slave to. You don't have to die young when part of your covenant promise with God is that He will fulfill all of your years. If you will be led, He will lead you down the path of a long life until you are satisfied.

Psalm 91:14-16 NKJV

> *Because he has set his love upon Me, therefore I will deliver him; I will set him on high, because he has known My name. He shall call upon Me, and I will answer him; I will be with him in trouble; I will deliver him and honor him. With long life I will satisfy him, and show him My salvation.*

Hebrews 2:14-15 NKJV

> *Inasmuch then as the children have partaken of flesh and blood, He Himself likewise shared in the same, that through death He might destroy him who had the power of death, that is, the devil, and release those who through fear of death were all their lifetime subject to bondage.*

Don't you ever be afraid of death. When you die—so what? If you are in union with Christ, death is gain. I'm telling you right now, I know I have a job to do on this earth, but when I finish it, I am ready to be with Jesus. On April 1, 2006, I had an experience of going to Heaven, seeing Jesus, and going to the throne room. When I was back in my bedroom, I was mad that I was back; I wanted to be back with Jesus! From that point on, if it wasn't for my family and the mission God has given me, I'd be ready to step back on over! The fear of death is ultimately what hinders so many people from walking in health because they keep plugging into a continual flow of death. So many cancers are the result of this; remove the fear that you revere and it will never control you.

If you are pregnant, you don't ever have to worry about having a miscarriage. Why? Because it's part of your covenant with God. You can fully expect for your child to be born full term and completely healthy. Why? Because we are dead to the curse.

Whatever disease comes down the pipeline—COVID-127, pig pox, elephant pox, and whatever other pox they come up with—I'm not scared of it. It is scared of me. It can't get on me because it can't be in my midst. If you want to be in a disease-free zone, stand near someone who is filled with the life of God and they know it, because my covenant says that sickness can't even be in my midst.

We must make the decision that because we are united with Christ, sickness is just not possible. When it comes to the next pandemic, who cares! My Bible says that no plague can even come near me.

So let's deal with reason number two as to why Christians get sick: their imaginations. This ties right into number one because this is satan's way of getting you to plug into the curse. He is wanting you to fill up on his thoughts so he can fill you up with the curse. It really comes down to what I call diseases of the soul such as condemnation, fear, and lack of self-control. Satan wants you to get your imaginations on all of the news articles on television and social media about all of the diseases that are in the world and all the things that are normal for the world.

In America, have you ever noticed you can't even watch one television show without seeing an ad for a prescription drug? How wicked is that! The United States of America is one of the two nations in the world that is so corrupt toward its citizens that they allow pharmaceutical companies to advertise their drugs. We live in a sick world in which people are so focused on money and power, they are willing to pump people's bodies full of chemicals and call it healthcare—and that's why so many people are sick. We just got through talking about our imaginations, so I am not going to go much further with it. But this is how Christians ultimately get sick: an unmaintained thought life.

The third reason people get sick is one people don't like to talk about, especially in America, and it is this: not taking care of our body, which is the temple of God. I will go into more detail about this in the last chapter, but I'll just leave this right here: if you don't take care of the body God gave you, it's not the devil's fault or anyone else's fault when you get sick. If you notice, ultimately, all three reasons are still tied to our soul. Remember, "I want you to prosper and be in health even as your soul prospers." How you think will determine how you see and, thus, how you live.

What about when Christians are in accidents? Well, it is simple—this will not be popular, but it is biblical—accidents happen when we are not being led by the Holy Spirit. When we stop listening, this is when we get into trouble.

John 16:13 NKJV

> *However, when He, the Spirit of truth, has come, He will guide you into all truth; for He will not speak on His own authority, but whatever He hears He will speak; and He will tell you things to come.*

This is about as plain as it gets. One of the jobs of the Holy Spirit is to guide us in life, reveal truth, and show us things to come. There has never been a righteous person filled with God who was in an accident and yet the Holy Spirit wasn't warning them. You will never convince me otherwise. Any of us who have been in an accident, if we are humble and honest, we can look back and realize that there was something on the inside of us saying, "Don't do that," "Don't go just yet," or "Don't go that way." He is always looking out for us, but He will never make us do anything.

Psalm 91:9-12 NKJV

> *Because you have made the Lord, who is my refuge, even the Most High, your dwelling place, no evil shall befall you, nor shall any*

185

plague come near your dwelling; for He shall give His angels charge over you, to keep you in all your ways. In their hands they shall bear you up, lest you dash your foot against a stone.

Who are the ones that the angels are bearing up with their hands? The ones who are trusting in God to be their shelter, refuge, and place of protection. Well, how can that be possible when I am not listening to Him? Friend, I am not talking about sin; I am talking about the daily affairs of life. Do you know how many times I have heard the Lord tell me to go a different way home while driving on the highway or to wait a few minutes before I left, or to do something different in an activity I am participating in? He knows the end from the beginning and He isn't hiding secrets from us. God wants you to be healthy every day of your life!

So with all that said, what do Christians need to do to walk in healing? Well, do the opposite of what you did to get the sickness. If we gave away our healing because we used our soul to plug into death, then we simply unplug from death and plug back into Life. Turn the valve of your soul and let the life of God flow.

Now I know that sounds simple. I like simple, and the Bible is simple, but what does this look like practically? Use your imagination and consider yourself dead to it. I don't care if it's a common sickness, chronic illness, deadly disease, or the result of an accident—consider yourself dead to it. Do what my friend and partner Johan from Belgium did! Use your imagination and see the light of Jesus radiating into your body. You don't need someone who stands behind a pulpit to lay hands on you. Christ lives on the inside of you! The Healer and all of His life is in you.

I will never forget preaching at a healing conference in Kenosha, Wisconsin, a few years ago. After I had finished my message, I began going around the auditorium and ministering to different ones. There was one lady who raised her hand and stated she was suffering with severe pain all throughout her body. She was dealing with a severe case of rheumatoid arthritis as well as other issues. It was so bad that she could barely walk even with the aid of a walker, and it took three men to help her get from her car into the church building.

As I began to talk to her and remind her of some of the things I had taught on regarding our union with Christ, she began to cry. I knew in that moment that there wasn't much I could tell her that was going to change anything So I stopped and said, "I want you to close your eyes and imagine Jesus standing in front of you." She was sitting in her chair and sobbing, but she closed her eyes and began to listen. I began to describe in detail what Jesus looked like, what His clothes looked like, and the light that was shining from Him. After each description, I would say, "Do you see Him?" and she would say, "Yes." I also noticed she was beginning to calm down and get quiet. After doing this for a few minutes, I said, "Now Jesus is about to touch you. Do you see His hand reaching out toward you?" And she said, "Yes." And suddenly, I reached out my hand and put it on her shoulder. She began to shake and then looked at me and said, "The pain is all gone!" So I had her stand up.

Now when she stood up, she was pretty shaky. I had to help her stand up. She was holding on to the chair in front of her and wobbled a little bit, but I kept holding her hand until I could see she was stable. Then I said, "Come walk with me." Now, remember, she could barely walk with a walker and it took three men to help get her from her car to her her seat in the large auditorium that also had a sloped floor. She and I stepped into the aisle and began to walk toward the front. She started out really slow, but all of a sudden, you could see her gait change and the congregation all gasped. It was amazing. She started walking with great ease, and when I saw that she was good, I gradually let go of her hand and we watched her walk up and down the aisles, doing several laps around the auditorium! She was healed just by getting her eyes off of herself and becoming conscious of the Christ within her and with her.

Friend, I have so many stories! Time and time again, I see people getting healed just by getting their soul under control and then beginning to abide in Christ once again. My entire goal in my healing conferences is to simply help believers understand their union with Christ and become so conscious of Him that if they do have some physical issues, they almost effortlessly plug back into life.

Now I will tell you something. If you are someone who has allowed your imagination to run wild and untamed for a long time, don't think taming your imagination will happen overnight. Abiding in Christ is not a one-time deal; this is a daily deal. To abide is to stay. The problem with most Christians is that we are just simply lazy. Forget not even going to church, praying in tongues, and reading our Bible. How often are we meditating on the realities of who we are in Christ? How often throughout our day are we considering ourselves dead to sin and sickness?

The reason most sickness happens and then Christians struggle getting free is that they only start going over healing scriptures and renewing their mind after they are sick. Friend, we are to be on guard. The way we stay on guard against satan is by maintaining our imagination and protecting our peace. Refuse the cares of the world and don't allow yourself to accept the world's normal. It's like someone who hasn't lifted weights in years suddenly being forced into a weight-lifting competition. I don't care if you used to bench 300 pounds, if you haven't lifted in years, you are probably going to struggle getting up 150 pounds! If you want to win in life, you have to abide in Christ, not go in and out.

If you haven't been maintaining your imaginations, then start now. But don't be surprised when a little demon comes along with the thought of, "Well, you know what the doctor said. There is no cure," or "Everyone else in your family has this disease, you are going to get it too," or "Don't you realize this is just a normal part of life and getting older?" To hell with all of that because that's where those thoughts are coming from! No, you need to cast those thoughts down. Remember, if Jesus doesn't have it, you don't have it. If Jesus can't have it, you can't have it. I don't care what you see or what you feel. Stop looking at and considering the doctor's report. All that worrying you were doing—instead of imagining what is going to happen when you die, start imagining what is going to happen as you continue to live. Spend time every day seeing that tumor dissolving. Spend time every day seeing your ear open up or that short limb growing out. See it in your imagination, and give your faith something to work with. You don't need to grow your faith; you need to expand your imagination.

Abraham was facing an impossible situation. He and Sarah needed a child, but they were both old and Sarah was past the age of childbearing. Do you know what God did to help Abraham? God gave Abraham something to look at; He gave him an image.

Genesis 15:5 NKJV

> *Then He brought him outside and said, "Look now toward heaven, and count the stars if you are able to number them." And He said to him, "So shall your descendants be."*

God brought Abraham outside of the tent and had him look at the stars and said, "This is how many descendants you will have!" It seemed impossible, but do you realize what happened every time Abraham was outside at night? He was looking at those stars. Those stars represented people, but for all of those people to come, there had to be one to come from him and Sarah. The stars became the object of his imagination every night. Those stars were reminders of the possibilities of God.

It didn't happen overnight, but eventually Abraham got the point that he was able to expand his imagination and began considering the promises of God instead of considering the impossibilities of his body.

Romans 4:16-22 NKJV

> *Therefore it is of faith that it might be according to grace, so that the promise might be sure to all the seed, not only to those who are of the*

law, but also to those who are of the faith of Abraham, who is the father of us all (as it is written, "I have made you a father of many nations") in the presence of Him whom he believed—God, who gives life to the dead and calls those things which do not exist as though they did; who, contrary to hope, in hope believed, so that he became the father of many nations, according to what was spoken, "So shall your descendants be." And not being weak in faith, he did not consider his own body, already dead (since he was about a hundred years old), and the deadness of Sarah's womb. He did not waver at the promise of God through unbelief, but was strengthened in faith, giving glory to God, and being fully convinced that what He had promised He was also able to perform. And therefore "it was accounted to him for righteousness."

Notice the word *consider*. Abraham didn't consider his body; he considered God. Your imagination is everything. I've said it numerous times and I will keep saying it—whatever has your imagination has your faith, or I can say it like this, "Whatever has your imagination has you." The seed that was produced through Abraham's body first began as a seed in his soul. If you want strong faith, you need an imagination that's filled with Heaven's possibilities. If you want weak faith, you simply need an imagination that's filled with earth's impossibilities.

There is another story in the Old Testament that doesn't get the viewing that it deserves. For me, it's one of the most powerful passages of scripture in the Old Testament when you view it from a new covenant perspective. It is the story of the serpent on the pole in Numbers 21.

Numbers 21:4-9 NKJV

Then they journeyed from Mount Hor by the Way of the Red Sea, to go around the land of Edom; and the soul of the people became very discouraged on the way. And the people spoke against God and against Moses: "Why have you brought us up out of Egypt to

*die in the wilderness? For there is no food and no water, and our
soul loathes this worthless bread." So the Lord sent fiery serpents
among the people, and they bit the people; and many of the people
of Israel died. Therefore the people came to Moses, and said, "We
have sinned, for we have spoken against the Lord and against
you; pray to the Lord that He take away the serpents from us." So
Moses prayed for the people. Then the Lord said to Moses, "Make a
fiery serpent, and set it on a pole; and it shall be that everyone who
is bitten, when he looks at it, shall live." So Moses made a bronze
serpent, and put it on a pole; and so it was, if a serpent had bitten
anyone, when he looked at the bronze serpent, he lived.*

The Israelites' sin brought disease into the camp. So what did God
tell Moses to do? Make a serpent and put it on a pole, and as long
as people look at it, they will live. Did you notice the Israelites were
not required to confess their sin to get healed? They didn't need to
make positive confessions. They were only required to do one thing:
change their focus. Can you imagine the snakes that were crawling
all over their bodies? They have snakes biting them and hanging off
their legs, blood oozing out of their skin, the infected parts beginning to turn colors—and God says, "Stop looking at your bodies and
look at the serpent on the pole!" That word *look* is not talking about a
quick look either; the word *look* in the Hebrew is the word *ra'ah,* and
it means "to consider, give attention to, and to have a steady gaze"
(Strong's #H7200).

Friend, if the only thing the Israelites had to do was change their
focus to be healed, why would you have to do anything greater? The
Israelites were sinners with a lesser covenant with God than we have.
They were slaves; we are sons. They were sinners; we are righteous.
Why were the Israelites not given five keys on how to receive their
healing, but the Christian is given steps, keys, and formulas on all the
things they have to do in order to receive their healing? Something
isn't right when sons have it harder than slaves! Thankfully, that is not
in the covenant of grace God gave us through our union with Christ.

Jesus never created you so you had to heal yourself. Healing flows from the Vine. Everything the branch needs, it comes from the Vine. When we stay connected to Christ with our soul, that is where fruit is produced.

Now, I am so very thankful that God is so very gracious and merciful. He has actually provided healing for the sinner by the life of God being imparted through the righteous. And God has also placed healing power, His precious life, within the righteous to flow throughout their body. But what do we do if we are having a hard time making that connection? What about the person who is on their deathbed? What about the person who is in such dire pain they can't believe for themselves? What about the person in whom something has happened to the brain and that person can't make the connection themselves? What about the person who is being oppressed by a demon? Well, thankfully, God is good and He has an answer. I would call it the silver healthcare plan, and this, for the most part, is for Christians who are living according to their senses and not according to the Christ in them.

James 5:14-15 NKJV

> *Is anyone among you sick? Let him call for the elders of the church, and let them pray over him, anointing him with oil in the name of the Lord. And the prayer of faith will save the sick, and the Lord will raise him up. And if he has committed sins, he will be forgiven.*

Once again, I want to point out the connection of healing and forgiveness. James, one of the pillars of the early Church, points out that even if the physical issue was due to some type of sin opening the door, that person would be forgiven. Done deal, case closed.

Now let's look at the main piece of this. Remember earlier we brought out that the word *sick* in this passage of James is not referring to a common cold or everyday issue; this is literally talking about someone who is in extremely bad shape. Notice the phrase "the Lord will raise them up." They are in such a dire condition they cannot believe for themselves, whether it is due to an accident, extreme pain, a mental issue, etc. The point is, they need help connecting to the life of God. So notice James' response to an impossible situation: have the mature people of God make the declaration of faith over that person and the Lord will raise him up. I want you to notice the faith of James. He didn't say call for medical help; James said, "Call for the elders of the church to pray the prayer of faith and there is only one outcome: the Lord will raise them up."

We need to get to the point in our Christian walk that we can be at a place of such sensitivity to the voice of God and such a consciousness of the Christ in us that all other options are off the table and we live in a place of absolutes. When I use my faith over this person, there is no other option—Jesus is raising them up.

What if we were at that place as the body of Christ that we had such boldness and confidence in who we are and Who we represent? Imagine the results we would have, the numbers of people who would begin to flock into the churches that actually believed in such things as well as the sinners who were in desperate need of help but now have hope. What if the Church began to walk in such a degree of our consciousness of Christ that the world came to us just like the people came to Jesus? If we would begin to walk in that place of power, the Church wouldn't have to resort to only giveaways of physical items to draw in sinners; we could have giveaways of the supernatural life of God that would draw in sinners and change their physical bodies as well as eternally change their spirit.

God is good and gracious. I have said it for many years and I will say it as long as I have breath, "God is good to Chad." Do you know what? God is good to you. God is good to all people. Just as God has provided sun and rain for the evil and the just (Matthew 5:45), regardless of the situation, God has provided healing for all people—healing as proof for the sinner and health as a present-day reality for the child of God.

CHAPTER 24

ACCIDENTS AND INJURIES

The vast majority of this book is pointing out the reality of this wonderful gospel of healing; this new covenant in Christ made us untouchable. In the last chapter, we looked at what God has provided for those who are in no position to believe for themselves, as this is what is addressed in James 5. One area that we have not specifically addressed is that of accidents and injuries. Why is this important? Because I know there will still be many who, even after hearing about the wonderful gospel of healing, will still say, "Well, what about when people get injured?" Well, let's address that.

So let's deal with the most important piece and yet most controversial piece: accidents just don't happen. Accidents and injuries happen for one reason: we were not being led by the Holy Spirit. Every Christian who has been in an accident, no matter what the accident, or experienced any type of injury, it is always and I mean emphatically always the result of not being led by the Holy Spirit. I know that is a strong statement, but the facts are facts because Scripture is Scripture.

Psalm 91:9-12 NLT

> *If you make the Lord your refuge, if you make the Most High your shelter, no evil will conquer you; no plague will come near your home. For he will order his angels to protect you wherever you go. They will hold you up with their hands so you won't even hurt your foot on a stone.*

194

To prove this truth, I want to first look at Psalm 91. In verses 9-12, God gives us the promise that those who put their complete trust in Him, no harm will come your way—to the point that you won't even cut your foot on a stone or, you could say, stub your toe! This is a promise of being untouchable. Think about this. God is promising not only will you not get sick, you also won't have any injuries. I know this sounds crazy, and if we didn't have Scripture for it, well, it would sound absolutely impossible. How is this possible? By trusting in Him—that means listening to Him as to what to do and where to go. When we do that, our angels are in a position to protect us from evil.

We see this carried over in the New Testament with the promise of the Holy Spirit.

John 14:26 NKJV

But the Helper, the Holy Spirit, whom the Father will send in My name, He will teach you all things, and bring to your remembrance all things that I said to you.

John 16:13 NKJV

However, when He, the Spirit of truth, has come, He will guide you into all truth; for He will not speak on His own authority, but whatever He hears He will speak; and He will tell you things to come.

The Holy Spirit was given to us to be our Helper and Guide in life. One of His responsibilities is to be our guide throughout our daily activities. In John 16:13, the word *guide* is the Greek word *hodegeo*, which means "one who is a tour guide; one who leads the way" (Strong's #G3594).

The Holy Spirit is like our tour guide in life. Where we are going, He has already been there. He knows the ins and the outs, the good places and the bad places, and if we will follow Him, danger may be around us, but we will walk right through it untouched. The Holy Spirit will help us to always make the right decision at the right time and always be in the right place at the right time. This applies in the area of relationships, business, ministry, finances, and yes, even in the area of accidents. If we will listen to Him, we will never be in an accident or injure ourself. Do you know why? Because He would warn us and say, "Don't go there!" or "Wait five minutes before you leave for work!" or "Postpone that meeting until tomorrow!" or "Don't step over there!" The Holy Spirit knows the end from the beginning, and He wants to protect you.

I will never forget an accident that happened when I was twenty-five years old and in my second year at Bible school. I worked at the Tulsa County homeless shelter during the graveyard shift and then would leave there and go to school each weekday. Well, one night as I was at work, I had this strong sense that I needed to leave work and go home. I had plenty of accumulated time off I could take, so I went and asked my coworker if he minded if I went ahead and left early. He asked me if I wouldn't mind staying until 6 am so I could help him prepare breakfast for all of the residents because there were a lot of people that night. I went against the witness I had on the inside and decided to stay.

Well, little did I know that a bad winter storm was coming through. Over the hours of 3 am to 5 am, the roads were freezing with ice and then being covered with snow. By the time I left work at 7 am, all of the highways were frozen over. I began to drive slowly and carefully on my way to my apartment so I could change and go to morning classes. As I was about halfway home, I was driving on a three-lane overpass with a car on each side of me. As I reached the top of the overpass, I saw a stalled car about fifty feet ahead of me. The driver of the car was looking at his tire and then looked up and saw me and two other cars headed for him. He took off running and jumped off the side of the highway. All I could do was hold on, yell, "Jesus!" and then I slammed into the rear of his car.

I ended up totaling my car and his car. The airbag in my car went off and glass went into my face. My eyes had so much powder in them from the air bag that I had to go to the emergency room at the hospital to get them flushed out. In the end, I knew this was my fault—from the stance that if I would have listened to the Holy Spirit's warning, I never would have been injured physically, nor would I have totaled my car and incurred a financial loss.

One of the things that resulted from that car accident was that I injured my hip and back. Little did I know that the impact was so severe that it jammed my right leg and caused my hip to be out of alignment. Over a few years, this caused me to have severe back pain to the point that I could barely stand for long periods of time without being in very bad pain.

After seeing a chiropractor one day, they told me the reason for my back pain was that my right leg was shorter than my left by almost an inch. They concluded that the car accident was the culprit behind the short leg because I wasn't born that way. The chiropractor told me there was nothing that could be done except for me to wear a shoe lift. I was angry about it but was in so much pain, I put it in my shoe.

I wore it for a few weeks, until one day, I was so mad about it, I threw it away. By this point in life, I was pastoring a church and we were seeing lots of miracles. I began to reason that the same life that was flowing out of me into others was also there for me. So one day while I was sitting outside and reading a book, I looked down at my leg, put my hand on my leg, and by faith released the life of God into it and commanded it to grow. Without thinking anything else about it, I went back to reading. About two weeks later, I was outside in the same spot reading a book and I looked down at my leg. I realized I hadn't been in pain for a good amount of time. I then realized that my right leg was the same length as my left leg! And do you know what? I have never had any pain again because the life of God grew out my leg.

Why am I telling you this story? Because God is a good God. Even when we sin and don't listen to the guidance of the Holy Spirit, God is not only merciful to forgive us, but the life of God is still always there within us to heal us from when we decided to be dumb. I couldn't blame anyone in that accident but me—but thank God for my union with Christ in that even in my mistake, healing power was still available to flow out of me and into my body.

God wants to protect us from accidents and injuries—even injuries in sports and at work. I love to play sports and work out. It is not only fun but is also a great stress reliever as well as necessary to stay in shape and take care of the temple of God. There have been many times I was going to do something and that still small voice on the inside would say, "Don't do that." I remember one time I was working out and was going pretty heavy on some shoulder raises. At one point, I was about to lift and I got the nudge within me to stop, but do you know what I did? I went ahead and lifted it anyway. Do you know what happened? I got a small tear in my rotator cuff. Now let me ask you the question: was this satan trespassing on my body? No, this was my stupidity of not listening to the Holy Spirit.

I remember another time I was outside building a barn for some of our horses. By the time I had begun installing the roofing, winter had started setting in. This one particular morning, I was headed outside to finish up the roof, but I had this inner prompting that I needed to just wait until the next day. But do you know what I did? My stubborn self disobeyed and climbed up on that roof in freezing temperatures. I wasn't out there but five minutes and my hands were like icicles. The result? I could barely feel my hands and I ended up slamming the hammer right onto the thumb of my left hand. Hitting your finger with a hammer already hurts, but doing it when it is cold is even worse! If you know, you know! Let me just tell you, there have been plenty of times when Chad was just stubborn and stupid, but every single time could have been avoided if I had listened to the Holy Spirit.

Friend, I know it sounds too good to be true, but this is the goodness of God. He is a good God and a good Father and the salvation He has provided for us is absolutely astounding. Even if you have been injured, the life of God is in you to heal that cut, heal that broken bone, fix your memory, or do whatever else is needed to get you back in tip-top shape.

Many years ago, while I was still pastoring in Texas, there was a man and his wife who showed up to our Easter service. They came in during worship and said that the only reason they were there was for a miracle. They had heard about all the healings taking place in our church, and they came to get their miracle. Five years prior, he was working on a roof and fell through some rotten decking; as a result, he broke his back. He had been through multiple surgeries and it had just continued to get worse. He was unable to work, had gained a considerable amount of weight, and could barely walk. Do you know what happened in the service? God completely healed him.

I guarantee that the Holy Spirit was telling that man, "Don't step there." The Holy Spirit is our guide in life—in every step and decision. He is right there with us every minute of every day. If we will listen to Him, we will never, and I repeat, never have an accident. God made us to be untouchable, but even in the times we allowed ourselves to be touchable, God is merciful to us when we turn to Him.

CHAPTER 25

FOOD AND DRUGS

I would be remiss if I did not address the issue of how we take care of the temple of God. I am not referring to the building that we gather in together to worship God but the body you and God both live in.

1 Corinthians 6:19 NKJV

> *Or do you not know that your body is the temple of the Holy Spirit who is in you, whom you have from God, and you are not your own?*

Even though God provided us a covenant in which we are dead to disease, many Christians are still alive unto it. Earlier, we addressed the three main issues that are causing Christians to unplug from life and plug into death:

1. We think it's possible to be sick.
2. We don't control our imaginations.
3. We don't take care of the body God gave us.

We have talked much about reasons 1 and 2, but I want to spend some time on reason 3. Throughout the world, we are continuing to see an increase in diseases and yet, especially in America, you cannot deny the fact that many of America's health problems are due to what we put into our bodies. It is becoming such an issue that I have begun addressing it. Sadly, there are not many church leaders talking about it, because, I understand, it is a sensitive subject. However, if we truly care about people, we will talk about what is needed for them, not just what they want to hear.

If you saw someone dying and you had the solution for them, would you withhold it from them simply because you think they will get mad at you? The issue is we have millions upon millions of people who are dealing with sickness and diseases that, in many ways, are self-inflicted. I have found that many people don't need divine healing; they need intervention into what they are doing to their bodies.

I recently had a conversation about these things with one of my dear friends, Dr. Mark Sherwood. He told me that God actually showed us what we needed to eat, and it is found in Genesis 9.

Genesis 9:1-3 NKJV

> *So God blessed Noah and his sons, and said to them: "Be fruitful and multiply, and fill the earth. And the fear of you and the dread of you shall be on every beast of the earth, on every bird of the air, on all that move on the earth, and on all the fish of the sea. They are given into your hand. Every moving thing that lives shall be food for you. I have given you all things, even as the green herbs."*

Dr. Sherwood told me that after the flood, when Noah's ark landed on the mountain, Noah exited the ark and received specific instructions from God. We point out in these instructions that God clearly gave authority to Noah over creatures of the earth, birds of the air, and plants on the ground with the clear guidelines—these will *all* be food for you to eat. Noah was neither encouraged to be a vegetarian, nor was he encouraged to only eat meat. He was simply told to eat all these things that God had made and created for him.

If we have predominantly the same genes that Noah had when he was given these instructions, and we know these genes are crafted for each of us by the personal hand of God, then these must be foods for us to eat to sustain the life of our bodies. Keep in mind, food is instruction with information that makes our genes respond and express themselves. These foods contain vital amino acids, fatty acids, vitamins, and minerals for optimal bodily function. Without these necessary elements, our body is destined to try to survive and run in a nutrient-deficient environment. Dr. Sherwood went on to say that approximately 90 percent of diseases they see at their clinic are directly related to failure to manage food, exercise, sleep, and stress.

I firmly believe that everything our bodies needed God created in the Garden and put into the ground. Our bodies came from the ground, so it would make sense that what our bodies need comes from the ground too—not a laboratory. I have a friend who recently told me about a health issue he experienced when he was in Africa. He had contracted a disease that was affecting his intestines. The doctors couldn't do anything about it, and he was going to end up having part of his intestines removed and have to live with a colonoscopy bag. Instead of having the surgery, he went back to Belize where he was working. He said over a short amount of time, he was healed—but it wasn't a supernatural healing. Do you know what happened? He told me that because of the pure foods that he was eating there in Belize, it restored his body. Isn't that amazing?

It was not God's design for us to put artificial preservatives in our food and begin to chemically modify them. None of the things man has done to our foods have been for our physical benefit; they have been for a monetary benefit at the expense of our health.

Look at the foods the vast majority of Americans eat: they are highly processed and filled with chemicals. A recent study showed that the higher the consumption of ultra-processed foods, the higher the risk of suffering from a combination of chronic diseases including cancer, diabetes, and heart disease—known as multi-morbidities.

> Ultra-processed foods are convenient (long-shelf life, ready-to-eat), industrially manufactured foods with added ingredients or additives (e.g. modified starch, hydrogenated oils)

that are typically found in fast food restaurants or sold via supermarkets. Examples are soft drinks, sweet or savory packaged snacks, processed meat, pre-prepared frozen or shelf-stable dishes, and more.[1]

In America, food companies have gotten rid of using cane sugar and now use high-fructose corn syrup. This is a lab-created sweetener that your body does not recognize. So do you know what it does? High-fructose corn syrup contributes to diabetes, inflammation, high triglycerides, increased appetite, and non-alcoholic fatty liver disease, which now affects over 90 million Americans. "It can even cause fibrosis or what we call cirrhosis. In fact, sugar in our diet is now the major cause of liver failure and that makes sugar the leading cause of liver transplants."[2]

Does that sound like satan is trespassing on people's bodies? I can't tell you how many people have come up to me wanting me to pray for them regarding type 2 diabetes. Do you realize that type 2 diabetes is self-inflicted long-term suicide? Satan is not forcing people to drink multiple sodas per day and ingesting horrible amounts of sugar.

Diseases such as heart disease, cancer, type 2 diabetes, inflammation, and so many others can be directly attributed to diet, specifically the increased usage of sugar and processed foods. Go back and look at the diseases affecting people before man took over God's job of food creation. You will notice there is a great correlation between much of the disease we see and the foods man has created. Why is this? Is it possible that we allowed the love of money to switch from what God created to what we can create?

People have even told me that it is too expensive to eat organic foods. Believe me, I get it. When we made a choice to switch to eating good quality food, I watched our food bill skyrocket. But do you know what? God is able to provide. Christians are doing this to themselves and then, after contracting diseases, we want to start using our authority against the devil. What we need to do is use our authority over our desires and use some self-control.

Galatians 5:22-24 NKJV

> *But the fruit of the Spirit is love, joy, peace, longsuffering, kindness, goodness, faithfulness, gentleness, self-control. Against such there is no law. And those who are Christ's have crucified the flesh with its passions and desires.*

God has given us an incredibly amazing body to live and function in and we have a responsibility to take care of it. It's not even ours, but God's; we are simply the managers of it. Three practical ways we can take care of this body are by giving it proper nutrition, exercise, and sleep. These are three things that we have absolute control over and are absolutely essential to the health of our bodies.

I am already getting into sacred ground, so let's go ahead and go all in. Let's talk about obesity. Can you blame obesity on the devil? I know there are a small minority of people who are dealing with some genetic issues, but for the vast majority, obesity is simply the result of lack of self-control. In America, obesity is continuing to become a greater problem. Obesity is a common, serious, and costly disease. Look at the following statistics from the Center for Disease Control in the United States.

- The US obesity prevalence was 41.9% in 2017 (March 2020).
- From 1999–2000 through 2017, US obesity prevalence increased from 30.5% to 41.9%. During the same time, the prevalence of severe obesity increased from 4.7% to 9.2% (March 2020).
- Obesity-related conditions include heart disease, stroke, type 2 diabetes, and certain types of cancer. These are among the leading causes of preventable, premature death.
- The estimated annual medical cost of obesity in the United States was nearly $173 billion in 2019 dollars.

Over the last decade, it is becoming an increasing problem for children. Childhood obesity is a serious problem in the United States, putting children and adolescents at risk for poor health. For children and adolescents aged 2 to 19 years in 2017-2021, the prevalence of obesity was 19.7% and affected about 14.7 million children and adolescents. For children, obesity also leads to breathing problems, such as asthma and sleep apnea, and joint problems.[3]

I am not bringing condemnation to anyone. Everyone has their issues they are dealing with and working through; some are visible, and some are not, so I am in no way being critical. What I am doing is simply telling the truth. We do ourselves a disservice to talk about divine health and all the spiritual side of things, but then neglect to talk about the natural things we should be doing. It's no different than in the area of finances. God has given us divine promises regarding prosperity; however, I can't keep charging my credit card for needless things and living beyond my income and then blame the devil because I am in debt up to my eyeballs. Why are preachers willing to talk about debt but not about diet? Both are the result of a lack of self-control, but only one will cause people to get mad and walk out. People are okay with you talking about their money but not about their body!

We must recognize the responsibilities God has given us regarding our bodies. We must be willing to put aside the junk food and sodas that have no nutritional value and are filled with chemicals that you find in weed killers, and we need to start eating the foods that God created for us.

Now believe me, I understand it takes more discipline to eat organic foods and it costs more money; however, why can't you believe God for the money? I guarantee you will spend less money eating nutritional food than you will spend at the doctor and spend on all the prescription drugs they will put you on in treating the effects of all the processed and poisonous foods. The sad reality is, people continue to do it anyway. Righteous people eat junk food, get sick, and then go to the doctor to treat diet-related illnesses while quoting healing scriptures.

Friends, it costs way less to be healthy than it does to be sick.

Not only have we looked to lab-created foods to sustain us, there has been a continued trend to look to lab-created drugs to heal us. However, prescription medications do not heal your problem; they simply manage the problem. Is it possible that even in this area, we have substituted brass for gold?

When God was bringing the Israelites out of Egypt and their 430 years of slavery, God was introducing them to a new way of living—living in covenant with Him where He was their Provider and Healer. Israel knew nothing about God; all the Israelites knew was Egypt's ways, including their sorcery, the occult, their gods, and even their healthcare. Over and over, God would warn them about turning back to the ways of Egypt.

It is interesting that not one time in the Bible does God ever mention doctors and medicine being a solution for healthcare. The only time we see the mention of someone going to a doctor is found in 2 Chronicles 16 regarding King Asa.

2 Chronicles 16:12-13 NKJV

> *And in the thirty-ninth year of his reign, Asa became diseased in his feet, and his malady was severe; yet in his disease he did not seek the Lord, but the physicians. So Asa rested with his fathers; he died in the forty-first year of his reign.*

I have found it oddly interesting that people preach all about King Asa's life of faith and lack of faith, except for this last part. If you read about King Asa, he started out trusting in God for deliverance against the Ethiopians, by whom Asa was severely outnumbered. Because of his trust in God, the Israelites gained victory over their enemy. People preach on this.

After Asa's defeat of the Ethiopians, he increased in finances and in numbers. When the next enemy came trying to defeat the Israelites, instead of Asa trusting in God, he made a treaty with one of his enemies. As a result of not trusting in God but trusting in his abilities, Israel was defeated. People preach on this.

But when it comes to Asa becoming sick and not trusting in God and, instead, trusting in physicians and dying, nobody preaches on this.

I must ask, "Why?" The answer is simple: people are scared to talk about it because modern medicine is so ingrained in our culture, people would get mad and ministries would lose money.

Now, before I go any further, let me say this: I am so very thankful for all of those who serve in the health fields. If it were not for the doctors, nurses, EMTs, and all those involved in every level, there are many people, including Christians, who would have died early deaths and gone to be with the Lord. The problem with this is the simple fact that we don't talk about how many people have died or been severely injured because of our current medical system either. It is estimated that around 250,000 deaths occur in the United States due to medical errors—and yet Christians all over the world want to claim that God gave us doctors.

Do you know that I always wanted to be a doctor? Absolutely. I have always been fascinated with the human body that God created. I think science is amazing, and I love seeing all the things that come from technology and how it can help people—but it was never to be a substitute for God. I'm not saying that all medicine is bad, but don't be in error and think it is healing you. I would dare say that in most cases, it is doing more harm than good.

If God gave us medicine, why did He not give it as an option in the Bible? We know that there were forms of medicine and doctors even back then. Why didn't Jesus refer people to doctors?

If God gave us medicine, why does it work for some people and not work for others? Why does it have side effects? Why don't most medicines get rid of the problem instead of managing the problem? If God gave us modern medicine, why do hospitals need insurance for malpractice?

Friend, we must accept what God has provided for us spiritually and yet also do what is needed physically. It truly is putting our faith into real action. We need to live a lifestyle of maintaining our imaginations, and we must also live a lifestyle of eating properly and exercising. Our bodies were made to move, and the sedentary lifestyles people in the United States are living are also contributing to a host of problems.

Not getting enough physical activity can lead to heart disease—even for people who have no other risk factors. It can also increase the likelihood of developing other heart disease risk factors, including obesity, high blood pressure, high blood cholesterol, and type 2 diabetes. The benefits of regular physical activity include improved sleep, increased ability to perform everyday activities, improved cognitive ability, and a reduced risk of dementia and improved bone and musculoskeletal health. Emerging research also suggests that physical activity may help our immune systems protect our bodies from infection and disease.[4]

Imagine how many diseases and physical issues would simply be "healed" if we simply took care of the bodies God gave us? Too many Christians are standing in healing lines for things they could get rid of by simply eating nutritious foods and exercising.

You can't pray to God to make you eat or exercise; it requires the self-control that He gave you as a born-again child of God. Daily we must make a choice to renew our minds not only to Heaven's realities, but also to God's way of taking care of His temple.

As my friend Dr. Sherwood states, "I see miracles of healing every day. It is the norm. Our people walk around well and have high quality lives. Why is this not the norm in the church?" That is a fair question indeed. What if many Christians didn't need healing for their sickness, but simply a change in lifestyle?

Notes

1. World Cancer Research Fund, "Ultra-processed foods linked to increased cancer risk, diabetes, and heart disease," November 14, 2023, https://www.wcrf.org/latest/news-and-updates/new-study-reveals-ultra-processed-foods-linked-to-increased-cancer-risk-diabetes-and-heart-disease.

2. Cleveland Clinic, "Avoid the Hidden Dangers of High Fructose Corn Syrup," November 30, 2020, https://health.clevelandclinic.org/avoid-the-hidden-dangers-of-high-fructose-corn-syrup-video.

3. CDC, "Childhood Obesity Facts," April 2, 2024, https://www.cdc.gov/obesity/php/data-research/childhood-obesity-facts.html.

4. CDC, "About Physical Activity," December 20, 2023, https://www.cdc.gov/physical-activity/php/about.

CLOSING

It is my hope that in this book, you see that through our union with Christ, God has provided more in the area of healing than we thought possible. The true gospel of healing is not health insurance for when you get sick; the true gospel of healing is that you have died to sin and, as a result, it is now impossible to be sick.

Even when we may miss the mark, God is so good and gracious in that He has provided multiple ways for people to get back into healing and health. Healing can come through the laying on of hands, declaring the Word of the Lord over the body, through cloths that have been filled with God's life, the prayer of faith, as well as simply tapping into the flow of healing already in you as a spirit united to Christ. In the situations in which sickness has come from lifestyle choices, God has given us instruction in the Word on how to quickly turn that back around and see health restored. Friend, the Bible has all the answers for all the general things of life. In the specific things of life, He has given us the Holy Spirit to teach us, lead us, and guide us—even in the foods we are to eat and the exercises we are to perform.

The Word of God is actually extremely simple; we are the ones who have complicated things by our unbelief and conforming to the ways of the world from which we were delivered. I beg of you to ask the Holy Spirit to open the eyes of your imagination and begin to see things the way Heaven sees things. See yourself for who you are: in union with Christ, filled with His life, and more right than any of the wrongs in the world.

Let us be the generation that takes Jesus completely at His Word, sees ourselves for who we are in Him, and allows the world to see God as He is through us. May we be the generation of the Church in which sickness and disease become a non-issue. We are the Church Jesus died for and became one with—the body of Christ that is perfect, mature, walking in the fullness of Him, and absolutely dead to sickness and disease. Never be sick again!

In Christ, we always win!

Chad

ABOUT CHAD GONZALES

Dr. Chad Gonzales is the founder of *The Healing Academy* and host of *The Way of Life* television program and *The Supernatural Life Podcast*. He holds a Master of Education and Doctorate of Ministry. Throughout the US and internationally, Chad has helped thousands experience miraculous healings; he is on a global mission to help the everyday believer walk according to the standard of Jesus Christ Himself.

www.ingramcontent.com/pod-product-compliance
Lightning Source LLC
Chambersburg PA
CBHW060756100426
42813CB00004B/839